Maths
for the
Dyslexic

A Practical Guide

Anne Henderson

David Fulton Publishers
London

David Fulton Publishers Ltd
Ormond House, 26–27 Boswell Street, London WC1N 3JD

First published in Great Britain by David Fulton Publishers 1998
Reprinted 1998, 1999

Note: The right of Anne Henderson to be identified as the author of this work has been asserted by her in accordance with the Copyright, Designs and Patents Act 1988.

British Library Cataloguing in Publication Data
A catalogue record for this book is available from the British Library

ISBN 1–85346–534–8

Typeset by The Harrington Consultancy Ltd, London
Printed in Great Britain by Bell & Bain Ltd, Glasgow

Contents

Acknowledgements

I would like to thank my children, Gareth and Bethan, for their enthusiasm and encouragement throughout this project and my sister Vera Perry who, in spite of a pending OFSTED inspection, patiently gave her time to help me with the original document.

I also thank Dorothy Gilroy for taking time to share her knowledge and expertise with me; Duncan Gilroy for his practical help and IT support; Janet and David Williams who assisted with text and illustrations throughout the book; Elizabeth Burns, Ralph Dicken, Ann Harrison, Marion Horley, Bernard Jones, Calvin Pinchin, Jenny Taylor and Pearl Wood whose views changed and directed the course of the script, and Ann Cooke, Professor Tim and Elaine Miles and the Dyslexia Unit, University of Wales, Bangor.

My thanks are also due to Suzanne Hamlett, Linda and Dan Holland, and Sue and Jonathan Wood who gave me an inside view of dyscalculia; and Colin Sparks who so kindly allowed his work to be used to help dyslexic students.

I also thank all my fine students, mostly from St David's College, too numerous to mention by name, who allowed me the privilege of sharing their joys and sorrows as well as their brilliant mathematical strategies, without whose help this book could not have been written. Last, but not least, Janet Gayler, who kindly took time to critically peruse the manuscript as she cruised the River Yenïsey in Siberia.

The author wishes to thank the publishers and authors for permission to reproduce extracts from the following copyright material: Vail, P. (1993) *Learning Styles* (Rosemont, NJ: Modern Learning Press); Levine, M. (1993) *Keeping Ahead in School* (Cambridge, Mass.: Educators Publishing Service); Qualifications and Curriculum Authority (1994), questions from Key Stage 3 examination paper.

In loving memory of Gwyn and Martha

Foreword

Anne Henderson was one of the first teachers in the UK to recognise the need to provide specialist instruction in mathematics for her dyslexic pupils. Recognising is the first step. Anne then went on to develop a philosophy, backed by materials, strategies and procedures for teaching mathematics to dyslexic students. She produced this bank of knowledge by the best means possible, teaching dyslexic students and using her special skills of listening, observing and evaluating. This results in a collection of appropriate and practical advice covering a great deal of mathematical ground.

Professor Tim Miles (1992) comments on teaching mathematics to dyslexics, 'To put the matter another way, if there is bad practice, it seems likely that intelligent non-dyslexics may in many cases survive it without any major disaster, whereas its effect even on the most intelligent dyslexics is likely to be catastrophic.' This book is full of good practice. It continually reminds us of the dangers of assuming too much about the communication of ideas and concepts. Anne's eye for detail helps to make the work accessible to learners.

The text, as is only proper for a book about dyslexics, is readable and liberally dotted with encouraging anecdotes. It is jargon-free.

Anne is an enthusiast for her subject and an expert and enthusiast for teaching her subject. This enthusiasm and the related positive tone encourages learner, teacher and parent.

It is particularly interesting to see Computer Assisted Learning integrated into the structure of the work described in this book. CAL will make an ever increasing contribution in the classroom and at home, where it can ease some of the potential conflict between 'parent as teacher' and child.

Anne's practical and accessible approach makes this book a valued addition to the (rather small) collection of books on teaching mathematics to dyslexics.

Steve Chinn
January 1998

Preface

This book is written to assist both teachers and parents who wish to help dyslexic students experiencing difficulties with mathematics. In 1973 I began to teach dyslexic students at the Dyslexia Unit, University of Wales, Bangor, working for Professor T. R. Miles. After some ten years of tutoring literacy skills to dyslexic students, aged between six and sixty, I was invited by the Professor to do some investigation for him with dyslexic students, who were having mathematical difficulties. As originally I had been a Maths teacher, often with large classes of students, the challenge was one that I could not resist. At that time little research had gone on in this specialist field so I approached the project nervously, having nothing on which to base my teaching. However, in time, I realised that all the skills I had acquired in helping students with literacy problems, consolidating basics, multi-sensory teaching, looking at learning styles and building on strengths were just the skills needed to help in mathematics.

In 1985 St David's College in Llandudno, a school that is well known for the way in which it helps both dyslexic and non-dyslexic students develop their own personal strengths, invited me to set up a Special Maths Unit. I was delighted to accept for I realised that teaching dyslexic students maths day in and day out was the perfect way to develop the best pedagogical techniques that would assist my students.

The prime aim, which has inspired the writing of a book, has been to document successful multi-sensory approaches, pedagogical techniques and appropriate computer software that have influenced me most in my teaching.

It would be sadly remiss of me if I failed to acknowledge the expertise of my colleagues who have given much support. John Temby, Sandy Ross, Ralph Dicken, Margaret Walton, Jenny Taylor and Nicky Silcocks all deserve thanks for their contributions and enthusiasm which have given me the confidence to write this book on mathematics.

Introduction

This book is not meant to be a syllabus or scheme of work on its own but to be used in conjunction with whatever programme is being followed in school. The National Curriculum provides an excellent structure for the teaching of mathematics. The main interest of this book is to guide teachers in their approach to each topic within it, for the maximum benefit of dyslexic students. It is written on the basis that the student is being taught either individually, or in small groups, for short periods of time. However, class teachers will find it useful to understand just what is taking place in the 'special class', and possibly find certain of the techniques helpful in class lessons.

The teaching methods recommended are those, based on my own experience, which I would use to help a dyslexic student with language problems. My teaching is always influenced by the Bangor System because that is where I trained. It is a flexible system which a teacher is able to use for students of all ages. If a student is six or sixty the framework and content are the same; it is just the method of approach that is different. I have tried to show that the main techniques in teaching language can be used to teach maths.

Throughout my teaching I use Computer Assisted Learning (CAL) to reinforce mathematical concepts wherever possible. The majority of students think that using the computer is the same as playing games on the computer, so do not realise that it is work. We find that students will come into the department to 'play' mathematics software in their spare time, which not only gives the department a relaxed easy atmosphere, but also enables mathematical topics to be grasped without direct teaching.

As with all my teaching of dyslexic students the necessity to be clear, to state each point concisely and to try constantly to use only small steps (which is not an easy task), has been followed throughout the book. In fact, I always advise teachers that to teach dyslexics successfully, you have got to teach the 'obvious'. For instance, a concept which seems clear to me as the teacher without an apparent specific learning difficulty in the subject (though I am acquiring one!) may not, for a variety of reasons be clear to my students unless it is carefully explained.

How to use this book

The book is divided into two parts: Part 1 deals with the language of mathematics, and basic concepts which seem to influence all levels of mathematics; and Part 2 deals with teaching strategies for particular topics that I have found helpful with the majority of my students. It is important to use techniques from Part 1 with topics in Part 2. Once a student realises that you are interested in the way he or she sees problems and you show that you value the student's opinions, then the student will relax, talk to you and begin to show you his or her often wonderful methods for finding solutions.

Throughout the book I have tried to discuss a difficulty and then suggest tried and tested ways that my colleagues and I have found helpful. Consistently I have shown **multi-sensory methods** that have been positive, incorporating as much **colour** as the student requires, using **audio tapes** when necessary, trying always to work with the appropriate **learning style** so that teaching will have maximum effect. It is important to build up a **maths dictionary** that is student not teacher led, for then it will be meaningful for the student. This records the topic, with a method the student understands, plus an example or two to show clearly what the words mean.

The use of **key words** to trigger a series of thoughts and actions can be beneficial. Each student will have his or her own preferred key words for every topic so I will not attempt to state which key words to use. However, I will occasionally show some key words I have used which have been helpful with some of my students. I have found that using an **alphabet box** to record topics is very helpful, particularly at examination time, because the index cards can be pinned on to walls under grouped headings and become a good revision aid. The alphabet box is for the benefit of the student and therefore should be in the control of the student. Teachers can suggest and demonstrate various methods for storing and filing information, but at the end of the day, it is the student who has to be happy with the information in the box and want to use it often. Some students find that an exercise book in four sections – Number; Algebra; Shape, Space and Measures; Handling Data – gives them the freedom to use related sub-headings to file appropriate concepts and topics.

I use the word **concept** to describe an idea, a process, or a simple cluster of processes which together form a related group. The word **topic** is one that contains several mathematical concepts put together to make a procedure. As we make progress in mathematics, topics group together, resulting in more complex procedures.

For example consider a question on the **topic** 'shopping'. If several items are bought with a specific amount of money, finding the total cost of the items would involve **concepts** of addition and/or multiplication and calculating the amount of money left would involve subtraction. As a student progresses there may be a 'shopping' topic question that includes a percentage reduction in price. To reach a correct answer a student would need to be skilled with all the previous concepts plus those concepts involved within the topic of 'percentages'. The level at which a student is working within a complex topic will show in the number of concepts required to reach an accurate answer.

Throughout the book the word 'mathematics' has been used to avoid any limitations and boundaries which the word 'numeracy' imposes. Tutors are described as 'she' and students are described as 'he' simply to avoid doubling up each time. The word student has also been used throughout as the approach I am advocating can apply to students of all ages, not just young pupils in schools.

I hope that teachers will find this book extends their knowledge about specialist techniques, and that parents will find it a useful book to 'dip' into whenever they feel they need help.

PART 1

Mathematics –
basic concepts and language

Chapter 1

An overview of the problem

Success in mathematics

For students who are dyslexic success in mathematics can be elusive. However when it occurs it can be infectious, because as soon as the student begins to feel its healing qualities, it permeates to other subject areas and he realises that there, too, he can achieve success. Once his confidence is boosted there is a distinct possibility that he will perceive that success in most subjects is just around the corner.

Not all dyslexics have problems with mathematics: in fact Steeves (1983) thought that many dyslexics were gifted mathematically. Joffe (1990) said that ten per cent of dyslexic students are successful in mathematics and 30 per cent showed no difficulties. However Miles and Miles (1992) state that:

> The overall evidence suggests that all or most dyslexics do, indeed, have difficulty with some aspects of mathematics, but that in spite of this a high level of success is possible.

From my own experience a few dyslexics can be placed in the dyscalculic category, indicating that they have got extreme difficulties with the subject. As for the remainder, there is no clear statistical evidence available to show exactly the nature of their problems, but, as with most students, their difficulties lie on a continuum ranging from mild to chronic, all varying in the way they are affected by their inability to achieve success in mathematics.

Thomas West (1991) says that for some dyslexic students, 'easy' is hard and 'hard' is easy. Many students seem to struggle with simple computation of subtraction and division, times tables cause endless sleepless nights, and even nightmares. Yet often I see glimpses of ideas and thoughts that border on the genius.

Students who receive the appropriate teaching that is geared to their learning style, are able to master concepts, then whole topics, finally moving on to more advanced work. They become enthused by the magic of patterns within mathematics and begin to love the thrill of solving problems. Sometimes we do not see this blossoming mathematician in school, but if we had the ability to see into the future, we would know that all our efforts to make mathematics exciting have not been in vain. Dyslexic students often reach their potential long after they have left schools and colleges, but it is usually in these places of learning that the spark of their brilliance was lit. Many seem to have potential that is somehow bogged down, stuck in the chaos of simple mathematics. If we can find the magic solution that sets them free, I am sure that the world would benefit from their potential capacity, that has been given the opportunity to soar to the heights. Enabling dyslexics to reach their own fulfilment in mathematics has been the aspect of teaching that I have enjoyed most.

Dyslexia and how it affects mathematics

A definition of dyslexia issued by the British Dyslexia Association (Augur 1993) states:

> a specific difficulty in learning, in one or more of reading, spelling and written language which may be accompanied by difficulty in number work, short-term memory, sequencing, auditory and/or visual perception, and motor skills. It is particularly related to mastering and using written language – alphabetic, numeric and musical notation.

From my own observations it appears to be a cluster of symptoms, which impede a student's learning ability. These symptoms include poor memory, sequencing problems, directional and organisational difficulties which result in students having problems in reading, spelling and writing. All these difficulties affect the mathematical ability of the majority of dyslexic students. They struggle with all or some of the following problems, which will be discussed in detail in subsequent chapters:

- reading generally in maths
- reading, spelling and writing maths words
- reading numbers
- reversing numbers and copying a number correctly
- connecting the correct symbol to the word 'read'
  e.g. the word 'add' means we use the symbol +
- remembering times tables
- remembering basic number bonds
- understanding place value
- recognising the decimal point
- using a calculator correctly
- understanding fractions
- understanding percentages
- estimation
- using formulae
- an inability to transfer skills from one topic area to another
- lack of confidence which slows them down ('I'll do it again to check')
- perseveration (e.g. looking back to check and copying the answer).

Pumfrey and Reason (1991) state that diagnostic tests for dyslexia (i.e. the Bangor Dyslexia Test (Miles 1982), the Aston Index (Newton and Thompson 1976), the Basic Ability Scales (1983), and the Revised Weschler Intelligence Scale for Children (WISC-R, which now is WISC-III)) all use items such as simple subtraction, recall of number sequences and recitation of tables, suggesting that the abilities which are also likely to be impaired are likely to affect mathematics as well as literacy.

Dyscalculia

The very word makes many wary of the consequences! However the literal translation means that someone is having difficulties with calculation.

Research by Gordon (1992) describes dyscalculia as:

a developmental lag in the acquisition of numerical skills, can be manifested in many ways, including inability to recognise number symbols, mirror writing, and failure to maintain the proper order of numbers in calculation. Dyscalculia may not have the stigma of some of the other learning disorders, but it is important that it be recognised when it occurs as a specific entity.

Hughes, Kolstad and Briggs (1994) state that:

students with dyscalculia have a diffuse impairment of their ability to perform mathematical tasks, a cluster of problems that is distinguishable from children with learning disabilities. The diagnosis of dyscalculia is currently imprecise; valid descriptions of, and well-delineated procedures for, remediation of this condition are needed.

Judah (1997), reporting on paragraphs written by students in Santa Rosa, California, says dyscalculia is:

adding, subtracting, multiplying, or dividing incorrectly, with seemingly small, 'careless' errors. Transposing and reversing numbers. 'Forgetting' to do something; somehow, coming up with other answers. Adding when you should be subtracting; suddenly multiplying when you should be adding. Somehow losing the process; not 'seeing' a problem to be worked on the page and, thus, not answering it. You can work the sample problem, but you can't apply the process to a slightly different problem. Everyone thinks you can do it if you try.

In my own experience, over the last 15 years, I have taught several students whom I would put into the dyscalculic category. These have been students who were good readers, mediocre spellers, often fairly fluent writers but their organisational and sequential ability, directional awareness and timekeeping were as impaired as their mathematical ability. Some have had their dyslexia diagnosed, not because of their poor reading, but the lack of mathematical skills.

The following quotes from personal interviews with dyslexics seem to highlight certain difficulties.

'When I compare my own ideas about a maths question with others I seem to be having information overload. I'm picking so much information up from the question it's like I'm receiving this information in not three but four dimensions!'

'When I am anxious my sight is so vivid and my hearing so keen they distract me from the question.'

'Concentrating on mathematics is extremely difficult so my brain takes "time out" and my imagination takes over. I daydream then.'

'Even when I try hard I make mistakes. Everyone thinks you're just careless and that you can do it if you really try, even tutors and that's the problem!'

In a family that I know personally, the mother and three children are all dyscalculic. She told me she did not realise that her children had a particular difficulty with mathematics, because she was like that herself. Once their specific learning difficulty in mathematics was diagnosed it was wonderful because it meant that they were no longer 'thick'. She said 'No more raffia or remedial classes'. At last their potential had a chance of being recognised.

Dyscalculic students do not only have to deal with mathematical problems mandatory in a school environment, they often struggle to become confident, competent shoppers. Dyslexics have told me that they find shopping a nightmare because they do not fully understand the amounts of money involved, so do not know how to offer the correct amount. As a result of this they like to pay with notes. They then end up with purses and pockets full of change, which is very heavy. The mother of a dyscalculic told me that she recognised her son's room in college by the little piles of change everywhere. He did not know what to do with all that change! His younger dyscalculic brother was told that the change was his if he counted it. Three days later he found out that he was £33 better off! The elder son, who is now a qualified chef, feels that he can never become Head Chef because then he would have to be responsible for the ordering and the budget which he knows he could never manage.

Families with dyscalculics have told me stories of days when the student has reversed the number of a bus, so ending up in the wrong town; read not only the time, but also the platform number incorrectly, so travelled a hundred miles by rail to a strange destination; or turned up on the wrong day at the wrong time for an important meeting. Helping these students demands a very understanding tutor who will try to organise daily, weekly and monthly diaries to assist in the organisational problems. Lots of colour coding will help with the correct reading of numbers, and the creation of meaningful rhymes and mnemonics, will clarify sequences. These students will also need all the appropriate strategies that one uses to help a dyslexic student experiencing difficulties with mathematics. However, on some of those 'bad days', when for dyscalculic students everything seems to be going wrong, their only recourse is to enlist the help of a good travelling companion.

On a positive note however, dyscalculics who have now left school, inform me that it is the little tips we have devised together which remain with them in situations when they need mathematical skills. One student can never be parted from his watch because that was the apparatus we decided he could always use to add, subtract, multiply, and do fractions on, as well as to use as a timepiece. When students need to remember particular mathematics when working, for example in photography, they will be repeating certain procedures, so eventually they might devise strategies to cope. One student takes hundreds of photographs instead of twenty, hoping that he will have used the correct measurements for at least some of those!

Chapter 2

Assessment and teaching

Assessment

Procedure

Initially a student with specific learning difficulties in literacy or numeracy is likely to be identified by either a class teacher or possibly a parent. Once the problem has been recognised, the educational wheels should begin to turn and the following stages of the Code of Practice will be followed. (*Code of Practice on the Identification and Assessment of Special Educational Needs*, DfE 1994).

Stage 1.   Concern about the student's progress is shown by a parent, teacher or the Health Authority. Information is collected by the teacher involved who informs parents and the Special Educational Needs Coordinator (SENCO). Progress is recorded.
Stage 2.   The student's educational needs are reviewed and if necessary an Individual Education Plan (IEP) is drawn up relating to the school's own mathematics policy as well as to the Code of Practice. Progress is recorded, monitored and reviewed.
Stage 3.   The SENCO informs the Head Teacher and the Local Educational Authority. Usually a specialist teacher from a support service will be called in to give advice and prepare another IEP if required.

Those students with extreme difficulties will proceed to Stages 4 and 5, when they may be given statements recommending individual teaching for a few hours each week.

Stage 4.   All evidence is collected and if it indicates that further assessment is required then a formal referral is made to the Local Educational Authority.
Stage 5.   A Statement of Educational Needs is issued. The Code of Practice highlights the importance of parental involvement: 'Children's progress will be diminished if their parents are not seen as partners in the educational process with unique knowledge and information to impart.'

Class teachers' assessment of mathematics

When a specialist tutor is asked to help a student she will know that the class teacher's assessment of mathematics is of great importance.
   The class teacher is:

- Probably the one who sees the student most and she will be aware of the student's strengths and weaknesses.
- The one to be contacted for any advice on background and home information of the student which helps a support tutor who is hoping to work successfully with a new student.
- Extremely valuable because she will still be teaching the student or still in school long after the Educational Psychologists and other professionals have gone.

Now is a good time to say that I do not think testing a student on the first meeting is a particularly good idea as it could make him hate the subject and you for ever. This is not an encouraging way to begin a tutor–student relationship. If, however, there is plenty of time to talk and the assessment test is not too daunting, then possibly towards the end of the session a short assessment could be carried out

Assessment tests

There are many assessment tests available on the market which can give a teacher a clear indication as to where a student is with regard to his mathematical skills. These tests enable teachers to compare student performances with those of others of the same age. National norms provide a comparative reference by which student results can be measured and evaluated effectively. Students who are performing poorly can be identified and more importantly their difficulties can be diagnosed to show exactly where a student needs to be helped.

As well as understanding the importance of selecting a reliable test it is equally important to identify the purpose for the testing. Sometimes it is necessary to decide if the tests are to be used in a formative or a summative way, or both. Is the test used to put a student into a particular class or to diagnose exactly where he needs to be helped? In the former case the test is easily administered in a group and the results taken into account. In the latter, teacher observation is necessary as is discussion with the student to talk through the errors he has made and try to discover just what he is doing wrong.

Choosing a test

The criteria which govern choice depend on several factors.

- The actual cost of buying the test.
- Age range the test covers – finding ones that will successfully assess all the students effectively (peripatetic teachers may be covering the age range 6–70!).
- Time taken to do the test. If, for example, the test cannot be completed in one session, various events (illness, sports day, school trip, etc.) may postpone the next lesson so that the time lapse makes the results invalid.
- Presentation of a test – no space to show working; questions badly spaced or poorly worded which lead to confusion; actual words used that are too technical so the student cannot answer; diagrams and graphs badly drawn.

These factors mean that choosing a mathematical test can be very difficult.

Table 2.1 shows the tests I have seen and used. The individual teacher needs to find one that she likes, enjoys using, is confident with, which gives her the data she requires and enables her to begin where her student actually is and not where someone else has suggested he is.

Table 2.1: Assessment tests for mathematics

Name of test	Details	Author	Publisher	Date
Basic Mathematics	Ages 7 to 15 Oral test		NFER–Nelson	1971
Mathematics Attainment	A – Ages 7 to 8.6 (yrs/mths) B – Ages 9 to 10.6 C – Ages 9.7 to 10.10 B – Ages 10 to 11.11		NFER–Nelson	1978
Early Mathematics Diagnostic Kit	Ages 4 to 8 Older students with SLD	D. and M. Lumb	NFER–Nelson	1987
Profile of Mathematical Skills	Level 1, ages 9 to 11 Level 2, ages 12 to 14	N. France	NFER–Nelson	1987
Basic Skills	Ages 16 to adult		NFER–Nelson	1988
Practical Maths	A, B, C Ages 9 to 12	Foxman Hagues and Ruddock	NFER–Nelson	1990
Sigma Tests	A and B Levels 1 to 5	Hall and Burke	Fallon, Dublin	1992
Staffordshire Mathematics	Ages 7 to 8.7	Staffs. Education Authority	NFER–Nelson	1993
Mathematics 7–11	Ages 7 to 11	Hagues and Courtney	NFER–Nelson	1994
Mathematics Competency	Ages 11 to adult	Vernon, Miller, Izard	Hodder & Stoughton	1995
Basic Number Screening	Ages 7 to 12	Gillham and Hesse	NFER–Nelson	1996
Essential Mental Maths Practice Tests	Ages 11 and 14 (On audio tape, 1998)	Graham Newman	Thomas Nelson	1997
Mathematics Progress Papers	Ages 7 to 11		Thomas Nelson	1997

Diagnostic testing

I find using assessment tests in a diagnostic way valuable, because it provides useful information. Observing a student whilst he is working through a test enables me to ask him what he is thinking when completing the assessment. If he meets a topic with which he is struggling I often stop the test and deal with that particular problem. Using the assessment time in a formative way helps to give the best assistance to the student.

The National Curriculum guides us so that our assessment can be specifically geared toward looking for difficulties within specific Attainment Targets. Assessment tests build the relevant categories into their tests so that records can easily be made as a student progresses through each test. We can identify for example whether the student is struggling with Number; Algebra; Shape, Space and Measure; or Handling Data. Various assignments and problem solving questions show the student's skills in Using and Applying Mathematics where he has to demonstrate his expertise in using apparatus, understanding our number system and making correct links between symbols and language.

Continual assessment

Continuous assessment therefore is of vital importance if we are to give these students the educational support they need. It is something the individual tutor is doing at all times as she needs to know just what her student has understood. She is watching for recognition in her student's eyes and probably for some physical acknowledgement such as a shoulder shrug, a nod of the head, a more relaxed shape of the body or even a facial expression that says, 'OK. I'm with you!'

Assessment recording allows a tutor to chart a student's progress as well as to evaluate her own teaching methods and resulting success.

Teachers should be aware that different types of presentation are important with different students. Some students may like to be taught in small steps, gradually building up their knowledge. Others like to sit, listen and watch as a whole topic is discussed and worked through to a solution, possibly encompassing several varying, but interrelated, concepts. Catering for the individual needs of each student allows a teacher to demonstrate her skills to an interested and enthralled audience. What better environment for learning to take place?

The M.Ed. thesis on 'Specific Learning Difficulties and Mathematics' of Pamela Holmes (1996), listed the following helpful points to look for in assessing pupils. Can they:

- say times tables correctly
- do simple computation
- say what the symbols mean
- identify shapes, even when turned
- copy from the board accurately
- make simple number sentences
- count forwards and backwards
- say the days of the week, months of the year in order
- tell the time
- read and write numbers to 1,000
- identify specific numbers from a set
- do mental calculations
- use money
- work out sequences?

Teacher observation

Written tests are not the only way in which students are assessed in mathematics. Oral and practical assessment, plus the correct type of questioning, allow a student to show his understanding of both procedures and concepts. Sometimes by providing tasks which a student has to think through allows him to demonstrate his problem solving ability.

Teachers are in the fortunate position of deciding exactly what they want from an assessment and are able to choose the correct test for their requirements. Sometimes a multiple choice test sheet will give the right results, it may be open ended or use constructional tasks which will show how much a student has learned.

A teacher who has the opportunity for direct observation is able to question in the right place, to gather invaluable information about skills and attitudes. Occasionally a teacher might find that to audio tape an answer and play it back to a student saying, 'this is what you said' may bring an instant response that will not alter what the student wants to say on the audio tape, but the discussion which ensues will probably stay with that student forever. The audio tape reinforces the concept that is being described by the student. Good assessment techniques enable specialist teachers to evaluate progress as well as to communicate this progress to the class teacher as well as to parents and administrators. Students too like to know how they are progressing and providing that the test is non-threatening then it can be of benefit to all involved.

Basic skills are developing amongst all students continuously but the rate at which they develop varies enormously. I have taught some students who learn quickly while others, especially those with specific learning difficulties, regardless of how motivated they may be, learn slowly. Students vary in the skills which they are able to use well, so certain methods, materials, books and pedagogical styles appeal to different individuals. It is the challenge of providing for these varying conditions of learning which makes teaching so exciting. Assessment tests which provide reliable information about the strengths and weaknesses of students' skills help a teacher to meet this challenge.

Teaching

Individual help

When a student and specialist teacher meet there will already have been much assessment. There may be a formal Statement of Educational Needs, a written assessment by an Educational Psychologist, a National Assessment result (SAT or Key Stage) plus a very important assessment by the student's class teacher, all of which should be taken into account by the specialist tutor.

If a student is given some individual help from a specialist tutor basics can be sorted out and the student can discuss his views on other concepts. He will begin to grow in confidence and furthermore start to make connections from one topic to another so that maths becomes a whole, not pieces of a jigsaw that he can never put together. Once he has had some tuition and realises that he has some self-worth, he will benefit from classroom discussion, feeling that he has valid points to add to the lesson. From my own experience students who are given just a little help on a one-to-one basis can make vast strides, whilst others need a great deal of individual help, and continual in-class support, right through their schooling. Once again, we are looking at a continuum which perhaps deals with students who require simply a little push in the right direction – rather than those students who really need help every day, before they can make any headway with mathematics.

Dyslexics in the classroom

The Cockcroft Report, *Mathematics Counts* (DES 1982), highlights the importance of classroom discussion. However, the student who is struggling with not only the maths concepts but also has limited reading ability, poor memory and is generally failing, will contribute little to a classroom discussion. If he is very brave he may make a stab at an answer which, when voiced, sounds as if he has not listened to the question. A considerable number of class teachers are able to give students feelings of self-worth and value their answers. Many, however, because of class size, overload of the curriculum and not least their own poor mathematical ability, are unable to consider the importance of obscure statements and 'bin' them without a thought for the unfortunate student, who will have thought deeply about his comments.

Some dyslexic students, when asked a question, do not give a measured reply, but go to the other extreme and into 'class clown' mode, shouting out silly answers to make the others laugh. That is how they cope with their dyslexic difficulties. This situation makes class teaching very difficult because of this irrelevant distraction which can spoil the lesson for all concerned. The teacher will feel angry and frustrated because the detailed preparation that has gone on is wasted, whilst the majority of the class has lost valuable time when both teaching and learning are on hold. Yet the dyslexic student knows that after the laughs here is yet another maths concept he has not grasped.

The National Numeracy Project

The National Numeracy Project was set up by the DfEE in September 1996 in partnership with OFSTED, SCAA, the Teacher Training Agency (TTA) and the Basic Skills Agency (BSA). Anita Straker, Director of the Numeracy Project, kindly allowed me the privilege of seeing the material which offers a formal framework for numeracy, which in time can only help the dyslexic in the classroom. It is currently being evaluated by schools throughout the country, so amendments could still be made to the document.

The purpose of the project is to raise standards of numeracy by improving

- quality of teaching
- schools' management of numeracy with systematic action planning, monitoring and evaluation.

The detailed programmes of study ensure continuity, progression and promotion of practical teaching strategies. The project encourages professional development for teachers, as well as family support for numeracy achievement. While this programme is not directly aimed at dyslexic students, its structured, systematic, sequential, multi-sensory approach can only benefit any student with specific learning difficulties being taught within a school that is following this system. In each lesson the language of mathematics is given a high priority, as is whole-class direct teaching which can assist dyslexic students. These students often struggle trying to discover for themselves what a maths lesson is about from words they cannot read. The plenary session enables a whole class to come together to discuss their work, generalise rules, reflect on the lesson and plan follow-up work.

The project follows the National Curriculum, so that specialist teachers will be able to use certain pedagogical techniques recommended in special lessons with confidence, knowing that they are interlinking well with mainstream teaching.

The document states that the programme is aimed mainly at Years 1 to 6 but, on reviewing the excellent material, it was apparent that teachers of older dyslexic students will find it valuable. The teaching and testing is ongoing until the year 2001 so hopefully in these ensuing years teachers and students will benefit from this comprehensive project.

Dyslexics at home

Parents of dyslexics frequently struggle to help their children at home. Often the student is tired, has probably forgotten the maths concepts and formulae he has been taught that day and probably cannot remember the exact work he is supposed to do. Allow him to rest after school to 'recharge his batteries' and become 'destressed'.

Parents need to discuss with the teacher the importance of:

- making sure a homework diary is used, recording accurately the work that is to be done;
- making sure instructions are read slowly, clearly, and that they are understood;
- allowing the student to 'verbalise', i.e. talk through his work;
- making sure notes are adequate;
- using audio tapes if necessary;
- making sure the right books are taken home.

Or as Ostler (1991) says

If none of this works, ensure that you have the telephone number of a non-dyslexic classmate who will have all the necessary information.

Kumon Maths

Dyslexic students can often be helped by having extra maths tuition after school provided by the Kumon organisation. This system was originally devised over 40 years ago by Toru Kumon in Japan. Godfrey (1997) states that this programme is not purely designed to complement and reinforce maths learned at school, but to develop the potential of each child by developing self-confidence. The individualised learning, which provides positive daily reinforcement is cumulative, structured, allows students to proceed at their own pace and improves self-esteem. Research carried out by Kumon Maths to provide information for the Dyslexia Institute, was reported in *Handling Dyslexic Students Effectively* (1997) and shows positive results for some dyslexic students. This document states clearly how dyslexic students can vary from the norm with regard to progression through the programme, but at the same time shows alternative strategies which could enable them to succeed. While this document is of great interest to tutors of dyslexic students, it was written specifically for Kumon instructors, to give them guidance regarding how to help such students and would not normally be available to parents or non-Kumon instructors.

Conclusion

Once a student's difficulties are identified then effective intervention can begin.

I think that if a student knows that his class and special teacher are working together then this gives him confidence. He knows that should he find any particular difficulty in his mainstream class then he can quite openly bring along his work to show to the specialist teacher. Then hopefully together they can find a way through the problem so that he will not only understand that concept, but also become confident enough to apply it generally throughout his mathematics lessons. This interaction between class teacher and special tutor allows for informal discussion and planning relating to the student's progress, as well as opportunity for exchanges of ideas. Very often because a special teacher has access to different resource material as well as different school situations, she is able to acquire new and varying knowledge to which a classroom teacher may not have access.

The classroom teacher on the other hand is an expert at working with a particular topic and indeed a particular group of children, so she too can pass very useful information to the special teacher. This interchange of ideas keeps 'doors' open, linking different information, and thus avoids the isolation described to me by classroom teachers and special teachers alike.

Chapter 3

Learning styles

Concepts in mathematics

Throughout this book a concept is regarded as a small unit in the learning process; several concepts together form a topic. Once a student understands a basic concept he can put it into the correct part of his brain's filing system for future reference. In time a student will have mastered many concepts, which in turn reflect in the vast number of topics in which he is competent.

Dyslexic students often have an erratic learning style, making leaps in learning when it is least expected. Some of my students can deal with complex concepts and processes without being too good at the basics. They may grasp a topic, then find a basic concept within it difficult and begin to fail.

Where a student is receiving help there can be discussion about what has gone wrong. For example, the error with the decimal place can be talked about and, if necessary, an index card made, which tells him that, each time he is dealing with amounts of money less than a pound, he must take great care with decimal places. This can be reinforced with several calculations and making sure that the decimal points are put in correctly and, when writing down, the points are lined up under each other. When using a calculator he must be sure to record that an amount under a pound is entered by always starting with the decimal point, for example:

3p entered onto the calculator as: .03
9p entered onto the calculator as: .09
16p entered onto the calculator as: .16
78p entered onto the calculator as: .78

Levine (1993) suggests many different kinds of concepts, but here are some of his categories which I have found to be helpful with my teaching.

Concrete   Those you can see, touch, feel, smell and taste (e.g. trees, cars, unifix cubes, geoboards)
Abstract   Those you can think about but cannot touch or feel (e.g. arrogance, infinity)
Process   Those that explain how things work (e.g. digestion, long multiplication and division).

Concept check-list
Level 1   I don't understand anything about this concept.

Level 2   I can tell you what my teacher said about this concept.
Level 3   I can tell you how I think of this concept.
Level 4   I have got a picture of this concept in my head.
Level 5   I can teach you about this concept.
Level 6   I can do my homework and probably some shopping using this concept.
Level 7   I use this concept in my ordinary life without any difficulty.
Level 8   I could teach this concept confidently to other students.
Level 9   I can adapt this concept easily and use it in different ways.

I use this check-list to see just what a student knows about a topic with which he has asked me to help him. If he is at Level 1, 2 or 3 then I know that I really have to go right back to the beginning and start again using scissors and cardboard, different concrete apparatus, more motor movements, more colour and computer software to reintroduce the topic in a more appropriate way for his particular learning style. If he is up to Level 4 or 5 I know that, while he thinks he has a problem because he has asked for help, in fact he has actually grasped a great deal of the basics. Possibly just a few details need to be discussed and worked through. If he is at the higher levels and has asked for help, it may simply be for reassurance or for some revision tips. A student who is regularly reaching the higher levels is indicating to me that he does not need help any more, and confirms my own thoughts.

Learning styles

The assessment of learning styles seems to be of great importance because, once it is identified, a teacher can be better equipped to cope with a student's learning disability.

Two styles

The test to identify learning style which I have used is from Dr Steve Chinn and colleagues' (Bath, Chinn and Knox, 1984) Test of Cognitive Style in Mathematics. A revised version is due to be published in 1998. This is an easy test to administer and gives a good read-out of style on the worksheet cover when it is completed. The identification of 'Inchworms' and 'Grasshoppers' is quite enlightening even for teachers who are often surprised to realise that not everyone else thinks and works through mathematical problems in exactly the same way.

The more I work with dyslexic children the more I have begun to rely on this particular information to help me teach. Not all students fall clearly into a particular category – some are in the middle, using one method to do one type of problem and a completely different one to solve another. It is the students at the extreme ends of this test who experience the worst sort of problems, who are set too rigidly into one way of working.

The main difficulty for the dyslexic 'Inchworm' is that he is unable to see the whole of a problem as he gets too bogged down with details (see Figure 3.1). Very often in an examination situation he will never finish a paper, thus limiting greatly his chances of getting a good mark. A 'Grasshopper', on the other hand, will 'leap' through any examination paper but will possibly have put down the answers only. He may have seen a question, thought of a way of finding a solution, probably used a calculator, written down an answer and then moved on. In fact on one occasion I actually encouraged a student to go through a paper writing down all the answers, and then to go back to the beginning to see if he could think of methods to write down which would fit in with the answers he had already written!

Two main issues seem to emerge from the Chinn test.

1. Inchworms and Grasshoppers do not think in the same way. Therefore a teacher with a different learning style from a student must be aware of the difference and adjust her teaching accordingly. Awareness of a different way of learning enables teachers to present material in several different ways, e.g. two-dimensional diagrams, three-dimensional pictures, information on audio or video tape and using computer assisted learning wherever possible.

2. Different learning styles require different resources to maximise the opportunities in a teaching situation. Teachers who naturally lean towards particular apparatus but know from their assessment that many students in their class will benefit from different apparatus (e.g. cuisinaire rods as opposed to multilink), need to practise their own skill before trying to give a dynamic lesson with the apparatus about whose capabilities and limitations they are not sure.

Inchworm	Grasshopper
Personality	
Prescriptive nature	Intuitive nature
Analyses	Holistic
Finds formula	Forms concepts
Looks at facts	Estimates
Has recipe for solution	Uses controlled exploration
Adds straight down	Reverses back and adjusts
Writes down	Solves inside head
Tends to do + and —	Tends to do x and ÷
Unlikely to verify	Likely to verify
Apparatus	
Number lines	Dienes blocks
Multilink	Cuisinaire rods
Counting blocks	Graph paper and grids
Unifix cubes	Geoboards
Paper and pencil	Attribute blocks
After Chinn and Ashcroft 1993	

Figure 3.1: Two different learning styles

It is important that a teacher is pleased with the material she is using. If for example a student needs to work with geoboards, then it is a good idea to buy a pack of work cards ('Actipack' Geoboard Work Cards (NES Arnold, Educational Suppliers)) and play with them at home. Prior to this I, as an 'Inchworm', avoided using geoboards because I could not see the endless possibilities for exploration that they present.

A teacher needs to assess what previous teaching the student has experienced so that she has a clear idea of what apparatus has been used before. Hopefully she will be able to ascertain what apparatus the student associates with failure. Then, by using different apparatus, she is able to present old concepts which have not been understood by the student, and achieve success.

This could be compared with having the right sort of reading book for the age of the student. It is bad practice to ask an adult who is a poor reader to read a book relevant to topics taught in primary school. Many early simple reading schemes do this. Instead, hunt around to find a mature reader, or even a magazine, which will allow the adult to practise his reading skills using texts with appropriate content. The Adult Literacy and Basic Skills Unit (ALBSU) offer appropriate texts for adult readers. In this way the adult with reading difficulties will not be offended by the material used, is not reminded of nightmare scenes of past failures and will be able to make positive progress.

Although I long to be a 'Grasshopper' and certainly try to learn some of their skills when I am working with them, under pressure I revert back to my 'Inchworm' state, relying only on my ability with pencil and paper to see me through!

Other learning styles

Whilst she is not specifically looking at mathematics, Priscilla Vail (1993) in her book *Learning Styles*, encourages us to ask students questions which are vital if we are to maximise our time with that student. Sometimes by listening to a student, sometimes by being sympathetic and making allowances for the student's emotional state, we are able to help. In fact we ourselves need to recognise the importance of 'talk' in learning mathematics.

1. Is the child available for schoolwork – physically, emotionally, intellectually?
- Has the student got a physical pain? If so, then I can do something positive about this (let him see the school nurse or a doctor).
- Is there some family problem that is occupying his thoughts? Has there been a family bereavement? Is a family member or a close friend ill? One of my students became very depressed on hearing that his mother's close friend had got cancer. When we discussed this sad event he said that he worried that his mother might get it soon. I cannot take away the worry but I can be understanding and make allowances for the student's emotional state.
- Am I teaching my student a concept that is too difficult for him to grasp? Do I need to backtrack further than I have done already until I reach the place in the topic that he fully understands? When I begin a new topic, I ask my student to tell me how much he has heard about it. I may ask him to teach me what he knows because I have forgotten what it is about, or we may begin to do a little bit of brainstorming to see what ideas we can develop together about the topic. In this way I can observe just where he is up to and can start from there. In this way he is not being taught material which is too advanced for him.

2. Does the child learn best through two-dimensional or three-dimensional material?
- This question puzzled me initially because I usually teach in a multi-sensory way, using concrete apparatus. Having read the question I am now more aware that some

students prefer to see a drawing or a two-dimensional picture. Computers are great for this type of learner so I have had to become much more computer literate to accommodate my visual learners.

3. Is the child a simultaneous or a sequential thinker?
- Does my student give me quick answers or does he like to go through a series of sequential steps to reach his solution?

4. Is the child eager himself to make connections – filing, retrieving, recombining?
- I translate this particular question as 'Does my student like maths?' If he does then he will be eager to solve problems by making the correct connections. If a student is given help at the right time, then, far, from saying 'I hate maths!', he begins to realise that he has some mathematical ability and finds that maths isn't so bad after all!

5. Does the child learn best with visual, auditory or kinaesthetic/tactile multi-sensory teaching?
- Whilst my teaching is always multi-sensory, this question makes me more aware that I should use first the student's preferred modality of learning to maximise teaching. I now try to ascertain through a series of observations which way he prefers and keep a record so that I can build on his strengths.

The computer program *Mastering Memory* (Mitchell 1996) is a valuable instrument for detecting modality strengths, as well as for improving memory. It is a good idea to ask a student how he solves problems:

Does he read, think, visualise, write, draw, talk, decide?

When he has decided how he problem solves you can make a logo with him (see Figure 3.2) which shows his thinking style. If the logo is made on the computer then he can reproduce it as often as he likes to remind himself about his personal style.

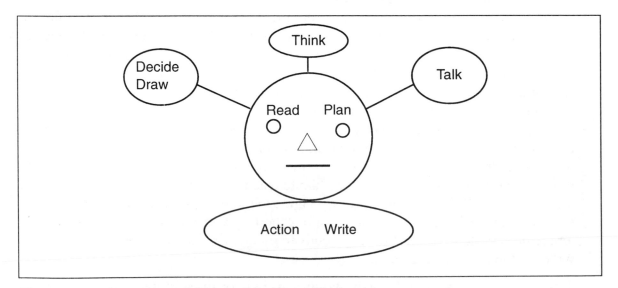

Figure 3.2: Logo to show thinking style – a problem solving approach

Anxiety

Students who are failing in mathematics almost always begin by telling me, 'I'm not thick, but I can't do maths. You see I can't remember my tables or what the words mean when I'm in a test, so I always come last.'

Most of my students at some time tell me that they are afraid of mathematics, dread the lesson and always feel that they will never understand anything. Dunn and Dunn (1987) stated that:

The mismatch of student perceptual preference and instructional activity mode appears to contribute to maths anxiety.

Battista (1986), and Larson (1983), said:

Use of manipulative materials for mathematics instruction has also been found to reduce mathematics anxiety.

And McCoy (1992) suggested that:

Even though mathematics anxiety is not fully understood, its roots may be in instructional methods that cause the student to begin to develop a dislike or dread of mathematics.

From my own experience other causes for the fear in mathematics are:

- Lack of basic skills with times tables, in telling the time and making simple number bonds almost always cause difficulties.
- Mathematics is a precise subject that most often requires one correct answer. (This does not apply to open ended questions.) Dyslexic students who are failing always seem to find the wrong answer. This means that they are almost always 'bottom' of the class and they become afraid of failing again.
- They become afraid of failing so begin to fear the lessons.
- Regular mental tests (maths teachers love them!) mean that they are being tested on all those skills they have not mastered, so once again everyone will know how hopeless they are.
- Mathematics teachers who think that dyslexia only affects literacy skills do not help to allay fears in the numeracy based subject.

If a student is afraid of failing then it is difficult for him to learn, because he cannot seem to concentrate hard enough on new ideas; so, once again, he is left behind and his anxiety about the subject grows. He fears that he is not only failing himself but also his teachers and parents, who are impressed by students who learn quickly and well. This is a particular difficulty for a student who, up to that time has been achieving quite well, working hard in mathematics and appearing confident. However, as soon as he has to demonstrate his expertise in manipulating simple number bonds or remembering the times tables in order to complete a calculation, he disappoints everyone. When there are too many processes involved, his anxiety inhibits his accuracy and in some cases paralyses his thoughts.

A dyslexic student will know from all the assessments he has had that he will have some problems with literacy during his life; so realising that yet another problem associated with dyslexia has raised its ugly head is sure to make him despair of ever achieving well in school.

A good working relationship

If a student is failing in mathematics it is vital to develop a good working relationship, preferably working on an individual basis with him. In a one-to-one situation the student often 'opens up' on all sorts of topics which are worrying him. Sometimes a discussion can enable him to see a way through a problem which allows him to concentrate more happily on the concept being taught.

An easy atmosphere during the lessons allays fear and actively encourages pupils to talk about mathematics. It also means that any difficulties within a topic can be discussed informally without pressure. Students who are relaxed will often stop me to show how they found a solution, or to tell me what they are thinking about, and share the ways they have discovered to solve problems.

Glen – Glen told me that he had worked out a quick way of multiplying by five.

- If the number is even, e.g. 6:
  then 6×5 halve 6 = 3 and add a nought   answer = 30.

- If the number is odd, e.g. 17:
  knock off a 1   17 – 1 = 16
  then 16 × 5   halve 16 = 8 and add a 5   answer = 85.

Carolyn – Carolyn said that she found subtraction difficult especially if odd numbers were involved. We discussed this further and she continued to explain that even numbers were ones she could easily manage. When we looked at specific examples I discovered that she had worked out a strategy which I had not seen before, whether or not odd numbers were involved. She simply subtracted the smaller number each time to avoid any 'borrowing and paying back', as she had never understood that procedure.

Example 1   81
                            – 36
- 6 take away 1 = 5
- 8 take away 3 = 5   (this is 50)
- 50 take away 5 = 45   Answer is 45

Example 2   727
                            – 358
- 8 take away 7 = 1
- 5 take away 2 = 3   (this is 30)
- 7 take away 3 = 4   (this is 400)
- 400 take away 30 = 370
- 370 take away 1 = 369   Answer is 369

Once this relationship has grown, students will come to talk about problems they are having with maths right across the curriculum. The teacher is then able to offer appropriate help or point them in the direction of someone who can help. These lessons should be individually tailored for each student and cater for his particular needs. This method allows for both student and teacher to work together in harmony, developing the student's skills so that he is able to deal eventually with varying levels of mathematics. It is always possible to go back to basics, regardless of the age and intelligence of the student, providing the teacher is aware that her approach is suited to her student's needs. She will need to consider carefully her pedagogical approach so that she actively encourages learning by choosing the right words and apparatus.

Short-term memory

I compare my pupils' poor short-term memory to a 'wobbly shelf'. If I can teach a little so that he understands and it is meaningful to him, then his memory 'shelf' is stacked in a level way and the knowledge will stay on it. Eventually, providing we can reinforce the knowledge, new information can be added; then the first part is moved to a stronger long-term memory bank from where he can hopefully retrieve it.

If, however, I teach him too much, too soon, in an haphazard way, building on my needs (for example, shortage of time, pressure of the syllabus, boredom with the subject) then his 'wobbly' memory shelf is stacked in a very uneven manner and almost immediately it will tilt and absolutely everything will slide off, so he remembers nothing. (Motto: avoid overload!)

This has happened so often that I think it is better always to go slowly despite other pressures; it seems more advantageous for my pupil to remember something (regardless of how little I think it is), instead of being taught whole chunks of material I think he needs to know, of which he will remember nothing.

Perseveration

Professor Miles described this to me as 'rather like a tune that won't go out of your head!' The *Oxford English Dictionary* defines perseveration as, 'the tendency for an activity to be persevered with or repeated after the cessation of the stimulus to which it originally responded, studied as an aspect of behaviour.'

In reality it is very frustrating because what happens is that a student completes a problem on a topic (e.g. length) and finds an answer of let us say 46.3 cm. He continues with the rest of the problems, looking back at his first problem to check, but in doing so copies that answer as the answer to his second problem. He continues in this way, doing different calculations, but records the same answer, 46.3 cm, for each separate problem. One very bright student confidently brought his work to me, completely unaware that five different calculations on Pythagoras had identical answers. He was angry that he had completed five calculations but ruined all his efforts by doing what he described as something 'mad!' In discussion afterwards with students we have decided the best way to avoid perseveration happening is for them to look back over their work, cover it up completely with a piece of card, then concentrate on the new problem and reach an answer before rechecking. This simple, yet successful, technique has saved a great deal of anguish with many dyslexic students.

Chapter 4

The language of mathematics

Dyslexic students who have difficulties with reading will almost always have problems with reading mathematical text. Mathematics books and examinations have 'word' problems that have to be read correctly or there is no way that an accurate answer will be found.

Reading difficulties

In mathematics careful reading is essential. Students who have been taught to speed read, scan and pick up contextual clues in English lessons have to 'unlearn' those skills when reading in maths because missing some words might result in relevant information being incorrectly interpreted. Students tell me that if a question is very long then they forget the first part of the question by the time they reach the end. Students with directional difficulties who are reading from left to right often do not see vertical tables if they are put into the middle of text and express surprise when asked questions about the table.

There are several other points to consider about reading, especially when it is concerned with mathematics. For many people reading ability is often linked to levels of intelligence, so these people will assume that a poor reader will definitely be poor at mathematics.

Reid (1996) points out that:

Most children display some level of variance in their performances in school between different subject areas. Children with specific learning difficulties, however display extreme discrepancies .... Such children may have abilities at non-verbal problem solving ... although their performance may still be restricted by reading difficulties, since some reading is usually necessary in all curricular areas.

Do mathematics teachers always know the reading level of a student? If he is still learning to decode then he will find some written questions in mathematics almost impossible. It would depend on the level on which he was working.

Do maths teachers always know the reading level of mathematics books? It is difficult to ascertain the accurate reading level of mathematics books because most readability formulae have been developed to use with literary text. Mathematics text is different as there is not usually the required amount of continuous text that readability formulae need. The flow of reading is not always right to left as questions often contain vertical tables, so this, as well as many non-alphabetical symbols, give false readings. A student who has difficulty with speed of reading, for whatever reason, will find his disability will affect his mathematics.

Many mathematical terms which are multi-syllabic (e.g. isosceles, vertices, multiplication) are difficult for students on their first encounter with them, but if these words are discussed and written down (possibly broken down into individual syllables) students begin to read and understand them. Making lists of words (see Word list, Appendix 1) and phrases that may be met whilst studying a topic is really helpful. If a student becomes accustomed to reading and analysing mathematical words, he becomes familiar with them and no longer is threatened by them.

Table 4.1: Maths phrases and words

about the same as	devise and extend	less than	previous numbers
across from	do simple tests	line of symmetry	prove and disprove theories
alongside	equal to	lower than	roughly
alternative methods	explain and record	make generalisations	select material
as many as	fair die	maximum size	smaller than
at the edge of	frequency diagrams	minimum size	stand a chance
at the top of	generalise	more than	too many
at the side of	give precise definitions	next to	too few
away from	greater than	nearly	the same number as
average contents	higher than	not enough	take a chance
be fair	in front of	notice the digits	use oral and written
check information	in the corner of	number sentence	what's the odds
check sensibly	investigate and predict	plan methodically	which display shows
design tasks	larger than	point of symmetry	with the aid of a calculator

Maths phrases and words

Reading the correct word and understanding the way in which the question is presented can cause problems. Apart from the maths words (see Table 4.1), the biggest problem of all seems to be with the non-mathematical words which are put into maths questions to make 'real life' situations. Many multi-racial first names fall into this category (e.g. Miranda, Sami, Morfydd).

Other non-mathematical words used slow the reader down and cause confusion. The following are examples.

Question 1   There are 16 counters in a bag, 5 of them are black. Miranda is blindfolded, then she chooses a counter from the bag. What is the probability that the counter she pulls out is black?

In this question the words which almost all my dyslexic students stumbled over were 'counters', 'Miranda', 'blindfolded' and 'chooses', showing in this instance that it is the non-mathematical wording which impeded the speed and accuracy of my students.

Question 2   The centre part of the spinner (the arrow) is attached to the centre of the card, which is shaded as shown. The arrow is spun. What is the probability that when the arrow stops spinning its pointer will be on the black section?

In this question the words my students stumbled over were 'centre', 'spinner', 'coloured' and 'pointer', emphasising the fact that the non-mathematical words hinder solutions. The word 'probability' was not a difficulty for any student.

Confusion with maths words

Mathematical words can often be confused with those same words used in a different context. Dyslexic students who are struggling with language difficulties cannot easily choose the correct meaning for many words. Here are two examples of confusion with word meanings which I have frequently met.

Degrees

Three Degrees	A singing group
Degrees	From university
Degrees	Measure of temperature
70 Degrees	Name of a hotel
Third Degree	Intense questioning
Degrees	Measure of an angle

Right

Right	Opposite of wrong
Right	Opposite of left
Right	Meaning 'Yes'
Right	Meaning immediately
Right	Meaning write
Right	Meaning 'Feeling fine'
Right	Meaning accurate
Right	Political Right
Right	Size of an angle

Is it any wonder that students become confused?

Students who have difficulty reading often see one word, but say another, just as, when they are reading a story, they might read 'rushed down the street' when in fact the actual words are 'ran down the road'. Sometimes the word they read is so near in meaning to the correct one that it does not affect the calculation, e.g. reading 'probability' as 'possibility'. However, at other times, the word that is 'read' is so different in meaning from the actual one (see Table 4.2) that it can make solving the question almost impossible, e.g. reading 'diameter' as 'diagram'. Often the student is too embarrassed to ask for help and struggles to make sense out of the question, becoming more frustrated as he fails.

Table 4.2: Actual word, word read

Actual word	Word read
continue	calculate
correct	calculate
algebra	again
circles	cities
paperbacks	plastic books
whose	whole
lies	lives
volume	velocity
value	volume
diameter	diagram
uniform cross section	unit cross shape
approximate	appropriate
recorded	record
category	calculate
frequency	frequently
classify	calculate

The following questions taken from a Key Stage 3 examination paper show just how confusion can occur with a dyslexic student.

Question 1 Mary, Arvind and Nesta wrote a mass to different numbers of decimal places. Mary wrote 1.7 to one decimal place, Arvind wrote 1.748 to three decimal places.

(a) Can both of them be correct? Explain how you decided.
(b) Nesta wrote 1.7474 to 4 decimal places. Can both Nesta and Arvind be correct?

The trouble with this question is the way it is written. The word mass has several meanings, e.g. a large coherent body of matter or a large amount or number. Also dyslexic students often struggle with decimal places. Many dyslexic students would read the words but not comprehend the question or connect the decimal numbers to the writing of a mass. Students who attend Mass as part of their religion will quickly be distracted (not realising that this mass cannot possibly be the religious one as it does not begin with a capital letter) and possibly give up on the question.

Question 2 They wrote a volume to different numbers of decimal places. Mary wrote 2.6 to one decimal place. Arvind wrote 2.65 to two decimal places. They are both correct. What are the lower and upper bounds of the volume?

The wording here is again quite misleading because for many dyslexic students a volume is a book which of course would have been bound. I have had students ask, 'Does it mean how many pages are in this book?'

Some ways of helping

It is difficult to decide how best we can help students who have problems with reading non-mathematical words, particularly in examination questions.

- If all examination boards asked someone who was skilled in teaching dyslexic students to look through each paper before it was published, easier first names could be selected and simpler naming words could be used to assist dyslexic students.
- Another alternative which was suggested by a student at Aberystwyth University is for examination boards to issue examination papers read on to tapes. Standard tapes could be sent out along with the papers, ensuring that all students hear the questions read in the same way, all hearing exactly the same emphasis – this would be fairer than at present. Headphones could be used so that students who struggle with reading would be able to play the tape quietly to themselves as often as they wanted and not disturb others. This would enable all students taking the examination to be together, avoid students feeling different or isolated, and would promote confidence. They would know that there would be no pressure to grasp the meaning quickly, which is when they make more errors than usual. Should students be able to use taped questions in examinations they would need to practise listening to taped questions for sufficient time before the examination so that they are used to this way of working.
- Students having problems with reading from books can be helped if they use a piece of card to follow the words across the page as they would do with a reading book. If there are too many questions on a page the student can either cut out a window in a piece of card to hide everything else or photocopy the question so that there are no other distractions.
- Those students who have good auditory skills could have questions read on to audio tape which they can listen to at home when they are doing homework.
- First names can be identified by one or two letters; in this way speed and not accuracy is affected.
- Highlighting and/or underlining important information can connect key words.

Spelling in mathematics

Mathematical words are often difficult to spell (horizontal, perpendicular, eight or ate? forty or fourty?) The following spellings are some that I have seen for the spelling of Isosceles triangle.

Issolise Trangle	I Cosalystryangel
I Sosileistryangle	Sausolees Hirangut

Here are other spellings.

vendirams	Venn diagrams
horizonl and fertpal hoyt	horizontal and vertical height
graf to thekwashun	graph to the equation
exanpul ovpyitayeras	example of Pythagoras

As can be seen from these examples, students need help with spellings in mathematics. The words should be given in a systematic, structured way that would link into the method they have been using to cope with difficulties in literacy. Teaching words in chunks or groups can help. A colleague of mine, Janet Williams, worked out the visual plan shown in Figure 4.1 to help dyslexic students with maths words.

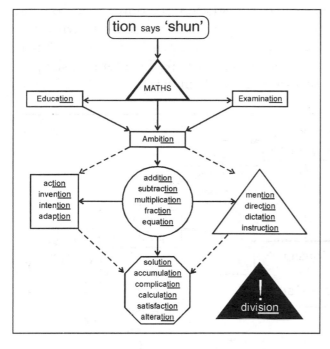

Figure 4.1: Visual plan to help with pronunciation

Obviously a phonic approach with dyslexic students can be most beneficial with spellings in mathematics. Other students might like to break down maths words into syllables and discuss their meaning as they do with words when studying English language (see Table 4.3).

Table 4.3: Analysis of mathematical terms

Word	Syllables	Meaning
Addition	ad	to, towards
	di	join
	tion	act of
Subtraction	sub	under, below
	trac	drawing
	tion	act of
Multiplication	multi	many
	plic	folding
	a	in
	tion	act of
Division	di	apart
	vi	seeing
	sion	act of
Fraction	frac	breaking
	tion	act of
Per cent	per	for each
	cent	hundred
Perimeter	peri	around
Prime	prim	first

Writing in maths

Although students seem to be rather reluctant to write in their maths books, they see benefits as soon as their attitude improves. Once they begin to write down methods they realise that they can refer to their notes at any time. They are able to use their own words and phrases to describe a procedure which they can understand when they come back to the notes later. They are able to colour and mark as much as they like in order to assist their memory. Figure 4.2 shows the advantages of writing in mathematics.

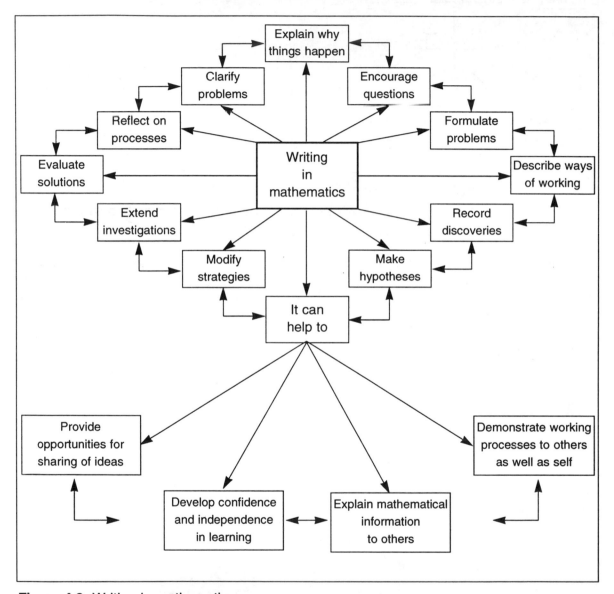

Figure 4.2: Writing in mathematics

Reading and writing numbers

Dyslexic students with number difficulties often cannot read numbers, even though by the time they are receiving help they will have been in a school learning environment for some time. They may be picking up more visual information to do with pattern and shape but basic numbers will be hard for them to remember. At this stage much practical work is essential – encouraging students to make visual connections and talking about what they discover and understand. At this early stage, a bead abacus called 'Sum-thing' is a piece of apparatus which can help students to understand the concept of number. The unique double threading of coloured beads allows easy manipulation, so that basic counting, number correspondence, simple addition and subtraction, introduction of multiplication and division, and many other functions, are clearly demonstrated. They appear to promote confidence comparable to that given by rosary or worry beads!

Only when a student is proficient with oral work, which usually is an indicator that he has developed his own understanding within himself, should any attempt at formal written maths be made. This step is important, particularly for an older student who has probably failed many times when trying to transfer from mathematics using apparatus to mathematics using written language to express the concepts on paper. He needs to be treated gently and guided slowly through this step if it is to be made successfully. Once a student is adept with simple numbers he can move on to simple concepts; then several concepts can be put together to make a topic. It is only when students acquire fluency within topics that the (wonderful science of) patterns in mathematics can be read and understood.

Some multi-sensory techniques to help students with number formation

- Making connections with apparatus for the numbers from 1 to 10. Some students need to connect the 'pattern' of the number to its correct numeral. The following patterns are seen on dice and are often helpful.

```
1 = *        2 = * *        3 = *          4 = * *        5 = * *        6 = * *
                                *                * *              *              * *
                                *                               * *            * *
```

 CAL program *Animated Numbers* (see list of software).

- Trace numbers from 1 to 10 in sand.
- Trace numbers from 1 to 10 on someone's hand or back.
- Put the numbers onto same size cards, noticing that most can have a starting point at the top as shown in Figure 4.3. This gives them something positive to hang on to.
- Drawing numbers on A4 sheets on top of sandpaper with a felt tip pen means that the individual digits have good texture for finger tracing when the A4 sheet is taken off the sandpaper. (This method may be helpful to teach other concepts.)
- Read, write simple numbers and use an audio tape to record the student so that he can play back to hear himself.

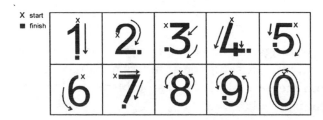

Figure 4.3: Writing numbers cards

Figure 4.4 is a simple chart and is an excellent teaching aid because it can be used for lots of fun activities. Use it to discuss and review our number system. Look to find exactly where each number lives. Discuss odd and even numbers and shade those specific number squares in colour and put the chart on the wall.

1	2	3	4	5	6	7	8	9	10
11	12	13	14	15	16	17	18	19	20
21	22	23	24	25	26	27	28	29	30
31	32	33	34	35	36	37	38	39	40
41	42	43	44	45	46	47	48	49	50
51	52	53	54	55	56	57	58	59	60
61	62	63	64	65	66	67	68	69	70
71	72	73	74	75	76	77	78	79	80
81	82	83	84	85	86	87	88	89	90
91	92	93	94	95	96	97	98	99	100

Figure 4.4: Simple chart for discussion and review of number system

Kumon Maths have an equally good magnetic board with numbers from 1 to 30. Students match up the numbers on the board with single magnetic numbered buttons. They can time themselves to try to improve their speed in putting the numbers in their correct place within the number system. This activity is similar to students arranging the alphabet letters in order at the start of a lesson.

Useful activities
- Search for row where all the numbers start in fives.
- Is there a column in which each number ends in twos?
- Make a game by saying, 'I'm thinking of a number that is bigger than 20 but less than 25, my number is odd and can be divided by three'.
- Have a competition to see who can be first to find the number 47.
- The 1 to 100 chart is useful for adding on tens. If I ask a student to look at the chart to add on ten to a particular number, he finds the answer but does not spot the pattern. In a short time he sees that the answer is always sitting directly under the number he started with. In this way we can then look for patterns when we subtract ten, add on nine or subtract nine and so on. Pattern spotting using this chart, calling out numbers, and colouring related numbers, is multi-sensory and most enjoyable.

Big numbers

Bigger numbers need practice. Practising writing cheques for large amounts of money improves both writing numbers in digits and in words. Bigger numbers need recognition from the right before they can be read from the left, which causes problems for dyslexic students struggling with directional difficulties.

Here are the steps we follow before we can read a big number, for example 23768054:

1. From the right split 23768054 into groups of three digits
   054   read as fifty-four
   768   read as seven hundred and sixty-eight
   23   read as twenty-three
2. Reading from the right after the first group put the word thousand
3. Continuing from the right after the second group of digits put the word million.

So reading from the left we have
   23 million   786 thousand   and 54.

It is worthwhile spending time talking about this procedure. Make a big card to go on the wall, as well as into the alphabet box, showing the importance in colour of the thousand and million positions. The 'look, say, cover, write, check' approach works equally well for numbers as it does for spellings.

Word problems

After reading through a word problem some of the following procedures may be helpful.

- Highlight, underline (whatever method your pupil prefers), the *important information*, just as you would do in a comprehension exercise, so that instead of seeing a mass of words, certain sections become clearer, offering a 'way through' a problem.
- If your pupil uses coloured filters or lenses, encourage him to continue to use them in mathematics.
- Once a problem has been discussed and a method decided upon, encourage your pupil to write down and highlight the *mathematical symbol* he is going to use.
- If a pupil is confident, encourage him to *estimate* an answer.
- If he is terrified of estimation (many pupils are) do a little together to show how easy it is to use whole or easy numbers. Write the estimated answer down and then with the student check answers on his calculator.
- Begin to work through a problem, use pictures or diagrams only if the pupil finds that this method helps. Several of my pupils have said that they find drawings distract their minds from the mathematics.

Chapter 5

Helping with basics

Use of practical equipment

The ruler

It is important to ensure that a student is using his ruler properly. If he is anxious about maths he may have sweaty hands which makes the ruler slide about, so it is essential to talk to him to relieve the anxiety. A student needs to know that a ruler has to be held firmly in the centre if a line is to be drawn straight. A discussion about the end of a ruler enables a student to realise that he must decide where to begin by looking for the first line from the end of the ruler, usually marked with a nought, and begin measuring from there.

Pencils and pens

If a student is writing badly in mathematics it may be because his pen or pencil is a poor shape for his grip. It is possible to buy rubber or plastic grips which help, from most educational suppliers. One student, Richard, whom I was working with, was so afraid of writing in mathematics that he wrote with his elbow touching his side. To move across the page he had to move his whole body – so you can imagine the state of his book! As he was left-handed I suggested that he pressed very hard on the desk with his right arm to see if that would help. He found that by doing this the tension went out of his left arm and his writing improved. I have been recommending this technique ever since and it has resulted in improved writing.

The protractor

Students usually like to use round angle measures if they are measuring bearings and protractors to measure pie charts and angles in shapes. The angle measures seem to present fewer problems than the protractors. However one student kept going wrong when doing pie charts, even though we had revised the method and he appeared to be confident. I asked him to complete the pie with me watching him closely to see if I could spot just what was happening. I saw immediately that he was struggling with left and right, clockwise and anti-clockwise when using his protractor to measure the angles.

Sometimes he would read the inside scale, then he would read the outside one. He was never sure which one to use. After we had had a discussion about this and made an index card with specific notes, he understood the method and did not have a problem with it again. It is better to pre-empt this problem by spending enough time discussing the properties of the protractor before using it.

Symbols of mathematics

The connection between the symbols and the words in mathematics has always been a problem. Gulliford (1987) says:

> there is a need to develop an understanding of symbols, so familiar and easy for the adult but for the child a further step from the real things and structural apparatus through which their understanding of concepts and relationships have been developing.

As I mentioned in *Maths and Dyslexics* (Henderson 1989) the use of diagrammatic connections has been a great help. The only difference is in the way the symbols are now shown because they correspond with the way they are displayed on the calculator.

I introduce the symbols one at a time with a young student. (With older students who are still struggling with word–symbol connections I may introduce them by showing all

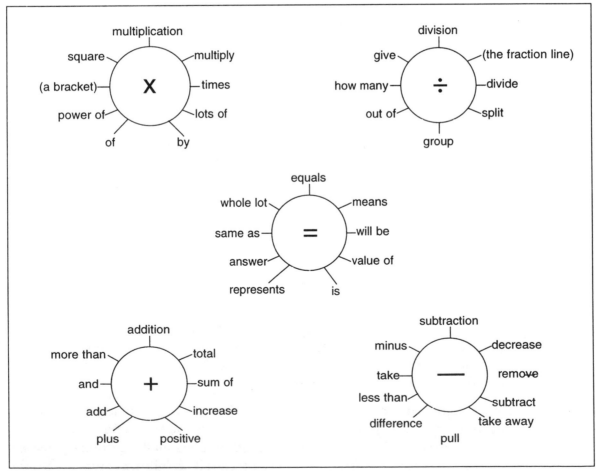

Figure 5.1: Mathematical language patterns

the symbols together on the same page and then discussing each one individually.) We draw the circle and colour it (see Figure 5.1). We then put in for example the addition symbol and about two words which the student uses regularly to describe that symbol which may be 'add' and 'total'. We then discuss what the symbol means and what sort of answer we shall find if we use the symbol. After much discussion we use apparatus to work out a few calculations, noting that the answer is bigger than the two numbers we have added together. If he understands well, we may proceed to record our actions. If he is struggling, we would probably go onto the computer to use a program that would help.

 CAL programs   *Amazing Maths, Maths Blaster – In Search of Spot*

We continue with the other symbols, noting the similarity between the subtraction and division sign but not allowing 'Miss, can I take the dots off the division and do subtraction as I'm better at that!' We link multiplication with addition, by colouring it in the same or a similar colour. The similarity of the signs is discussed and then we have a practical demonstration of how multiplication is a quick way of doing addition and how that sign too gives bigger answers.

Once students have become proficient with these symbols and more confident with mathematics, it is possible to tell them that when we multiply with a number less than one, the answer, in fact, is smaller, and, likewise, when we divide with a number less than one, the answer is bigger. I speak from experience when I say that you must choose your time with care to do this or much confusion will ensue.

The equals sign is very important so needs a colour of its own. Students using calculators do not realise that the = sign on the calculator means equals. They simply press the button that gives them the answer. They need to talk about the equal balance that is on each side of an equation:

e.g. $3 + 5 = 8$ $8 - 5 = 3$ $8 - 3 = 5$

If students are taught this when they are young, it appears to help them later on when they have to deal with equations in all subjects right across the curriculum.

 CAL programs   *Amazing Maths, Connections, Ten out of Ten Essential Maths, Best Four Maths, Hooray for Henrietta, Sum-Thing, Number Cruncher, Table Aliens* (see list of software)

Times tables

'Once I knew all my tables but I can't remember any of them now!'

Dyslexics find difficulty in remembering their tables but for many it is not a problem because they have devised reliable strategies to reach the answer. Others can be taught strategies which help, such as building on to easy tables (like twos, fives and tens) to work out answers. Chinn (1996) and Henderson (1989) suggest many ways of helping with tables but here are other methods that may help.

1. Stick a table square on to card and then make this L-shaped card to help with reading the square (see Figure 5.2). This L-shape was devised when some students kept reading the square wrongly. When a student is starting his maths dictionary, make a pocket on the front cover (by sticking on a piece of card with sellotape) where the table square plus the L-shaped card can sit for easy access.

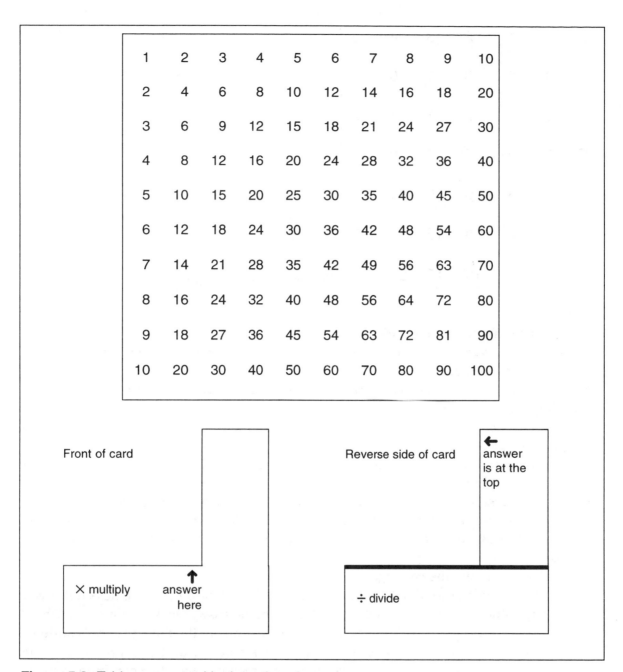

Figure 5.2: Table square and L-shaped card

2. This method begins with positive reinforcement. Two identical small table squares are made (see Figure 5.3) and both tutor and student have one.

   For each multiplication fact that is shown, a blank playing card is made, with that fact written on one side. From this small table square the facts will be:

0 × 0	0 × 1, 1 × 0	0 × 2, 2 × 0	0 × 3, 3 × 0	0 × 4, 4 × 0	0 × 5, 5 × 0
1 × 1	1 × 2, 2 × 1	1 × 3, 3 × 1	1 × 4, 4 × 1	1 × 5, 5 × 1	
2 × 2	2 × 3, 3 × 2	2 × 4, 4 × 2	2 × 5, 5 × 2		
3 × 3	3 × 4, 4 × 3	3 × 5, 5 × 3			
4 × 4	4 × 5, 5 × 4				
5 × 5					

	0	1	2	3	4	5
0	0	0	0	0	0	0
1	0	1	2	3	4	5
2	0	2	4	6	8	10
3	0	3	6	9	12	15
4	0	4	8	12	16	20
5	0	5	10	15	20	25

Figure 5.3: A table square

Method
- The card is shown to the student, e.g. 1 × 3.
- If he knows the answer then he is given the card and he highlights the square 1 × 3 in his favourite colour.
- This procedure is repeated with each card being given and the square being highlighted every time the answer is known.
- If a multiplication fact, e.g. 4 × 3, is not known, then the card is not given and the square remains blank.
- The multiplication fact is discussed and the student is encouraged to talk about how he would find the answer.
- On the reverse side of the card we put his own personal logo (see page 18) to remind him how he thinks, in addition to the way he has decided that he can work out the answer. In this case it may be 2 × 3 and double the answer. *We do not write down the answer.*
- Later, he is shown the card again:
  (a) If he knows the answer, he receives a tick. When the card has three ticks it is given to the student who then proceeds to highlight the answer to 4 × 3. Once the whole of this table square is highlighted then the next line of the table square is added.
  (b) If he does not know the answer, then we look together at the reverse side of the card to see how to find the answer to jog his memory and then continue as in (a) above.
  A student who highlights all of one part of the table square is delighted with his progress and is keen to learn and colour the next row.
3. Table audio tapes can be bought to help. Listen to the audio tapes before buying them because some tunes are more easily remembered than others. Video tapes can help but are more easily accessed at home than in school.
4. Allow a student to create a blank table square on the computer. He then has to think carefully about each number before filling in the answers. Most students see that they only need to think about half the square as there is a line of symmetry diagonally across the square. They can do the mirror image very quickly to complete the square. Then they have a neat, accurate table square which they are proud to show to everyone as well as sticking it into their books. This method has had very good results

with regard to helping students remember times tables.

5. Plastic table squares, the size of a cash card and called 'Check Cards', are useful as they can be put into wallets for easy, quick reference. (See Resources section.)

6. Triangles such as those shown in Figure 5.4 enable pupils to practise multiplication. In triangle A the pupil places his answer to 4 × 2 in the empty box. Then answers should be placed in the three empty boxes in triangle B (e.g. 2 × 10 = 20). In C, the pupil places his answers in the circles.

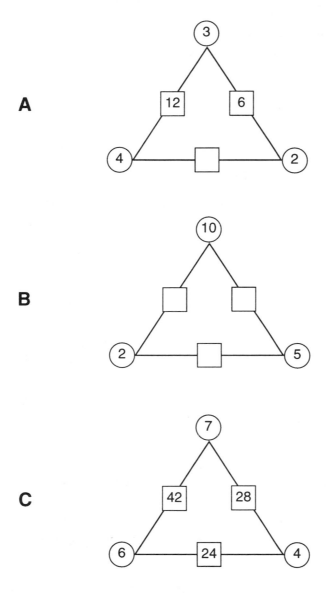

Figure 5.4: Triangles for practising multiplication

Place value

Place value is an abstract concept that can only be introduced when students are competent with adding numbers together.

Orton (1992) discusses place value in detail, and states that

Considering that our present number system did take a long time to develop it should not be surprising that some of our children are very slow to grasp the full implications of the notation and its underlying conceptual structure.

Hart *et al.* (1981) cited the following example, which acted as a useful guide to test a student's understanding of place value:

A meter registering the number of people going into a football stand was showing 06399. After one more person what did the meter register?

Groups of ten can be shown well with Dienes Blocks, multilink or a simple abacus. Students are able to use our money system to develop their understanding of the decimal system, but, as was shown from the information on dyscalculics, they in fact rarely find our money system easy.

Older students who appear to be confident with easy numbers often cannot recognise a number when asked to read it aloud. If asked specifically the size a particular digit is representing within a larger number they tend to struggle to reach an answer; for example,

7402 – What is the value of the 4 in this number?

Dyslexics who are struggling with mathematics appear to find exercises like adding on 10 difficult (for example, What is 10 more than 196? What is 10 more than 521?).

It is a good idea to practise a few of these problems as a start to a lesson. Place value becomes a big obstacle when students have to multiply or divide numbers by 10, 100 or 1,000. Many teachers think this is an easy exercise but I have had students come to see me in tears bcause they could not grasp the mechanics of this computation. A computer program that has proved helpful is 'Tenners' on the Smile software package. We have also found 'Arrow Cards', which are easily made out of cardboard, helpful.

The cards, which are a series of hundreds, tens, units, tenths and hundredths each ranging from 0 to 9, fit together cleverly to show place value. These cards show the decimal point position very well. Even if a student tries to put, for example, a hundred in the wrong place, then the cards will not fit together properly. It is like trying to push a piece of a jigsaw puzzle into the wrong place.

Students can be helped by:

- using the 'Tenners' program (Smile Mathematics, see section listing software)
- using Arrow cards
- playing the 'Place Value' game (Taskmaster, see Resources section for addresses)
- talking about the problem, using colour to make hundreds, tens and units look different
- encouraged practice in a friendly way.

Estimation and approximation

This is a skill that is useful not only in school but all through life.

Recently I was asked to assess an adult because her employers were concerned about her bookkeeping. She displayed excellent techniques in mathematics but had very poor estimation skills. This deficiency was causing havoc, with not only the tills in the shop, but

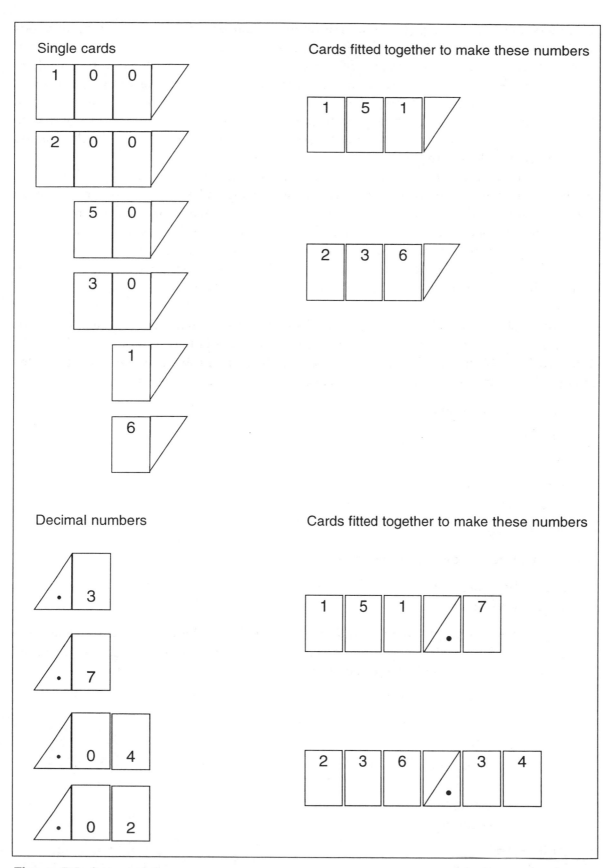

Figure 5.5: Arrow cards

the orders she was placing, as they bore little resemblance to the correct amount of goods she should have been ordering. She thought that because she had never had difficulties with mathematics in school, having achieved a grade C in her GCSE examination, there was no need for her to double check her answers on a calculator. In fact her dyslexia was diagnosed at this late date because her extreme problems with spelling 'came to light' in this assessment. She was given help with spellings and given a different role at work, so that she could use her excellent interpersonal skills with customers, which enabled someone else to deal with finances.

I very often estimate roughly how much milk I will need if I am having visitors, how much time it will take to go to a meeting, or how many miles it is to a nearby town. In school, estimation allows a pupil to know the approximate size of an answer. If he is using a calculator he can check that the 'correct' answer shown on the display is roughly the right size by referring to his estimate. It is good practice to divide a page into two, using one half to do the estimates and the other half for the accurate answer. Students then acquire the habit of doing a quick estimate each time they are doing a mathematical calculation.

Many dyslexics are loathe to estimate. Often when I suggest that we do some approximation, I am told that 'using the proper numbers is hard enough so why make things difficult by using others, as well as doing the same problem twice!' In spite of the protestations, I try as early as possible to encourage my pupils to estimate answers.

At first use easy numbers

18 + 34
20 + 30 = 50

Ignore decimal points

23.2 + 48.6
20 + 50 = 70

Later encourage a more precise estimate

24.5   becomes   25
102.3   becomes   102

Once a pupil acquires the skill of estimation there are different levels he can move on to so that eventually he is doing 'advanced' estimation which means his answers can be relied upon even for quite complicated calculations.

Using easy and whole numbers

43 + 97
40 + 100   estimate 140
            accurate 140

1.9 × 4.2
2   × 4   estimate 8
            accurate 7.98

41.06 ÷ 3.6
40 ÷ 4   estimate 10
            accurate 11.41

Multiplying big numbers

238×591
200×600
Count the noughts and put them in the answer 0000
$2 \times 6 = 12$ put that in the answer   120000 Estimate   Accurate 140658

Dividing big numbers

$923 \div 26$
$900 \div 30$
Cross off noughts equally in each number (1 in each in this example)
Estimate $90 \div 3 = 30$ Accurate 35.5

Practical applications of estimation

(A) Using easy numbers
Easy numbers are a quick and easy way of finding an estimate.

Question   John is asked to estimate how much stock there is in the food shop where he works. He starts with cans of soup. He could begin to count but because that would take too long and only an approximation is required, he estimates. Tins are stacked 7 deep and 48 across on each shelf. There are nine shelves.

Using easy numbers: 7 shelves   48 across
Each shelf has   6 $\times$ 50 cans   300 cans
   (7 is a difficult times table to remember so use 6)
9 shelves (say 10)   approximation   300 $\times$ 10 = 3000 cans
   Correct number of cans   =   3024

(B) Rough estimate
A rough estimation of an answer is often needed quickly. Ask, 'Is the estimate higher or lower than the accurate answer?'

Questions on hire purchase.
   To buy a portable stereo
      26 weeks at £1.97   Is this more than £50 or less?
   To buy a bike
      36 months at £9.96   Is this more than £400?

(C) Making an educated guess
Often approximations are related to the context of the question. So to make an educated guess or work out a quick, fairly accurate estimate depends on the amount of money or quantity involved. Sometimes, it is necessary to round off to the nearest penny, but at other times an estimate to the nearest thousand is good enough for the problem that is being considered. The larger the amount usually means a more general estimate can be given. This can be seen in the following questions.

1. The cost of materials to decorate a room
   £264.72 – Estimate £270
2. The estimated cost to build a garage
   £5,640 – Estimate £6,000
3. The price of a car (make, style, etc?)
   £12,858 – Estimate £13,000
4. The cost of material to make a dress
   £14.38 – Estimate £14.50
5. House prices in a particular area
   £26,840 – £96,325
   cheapest   *dearest*
   £30,000 – £100,000

Life after school is full of estimation.
Travelling by taxi at a charge of 42p a mile

 CAL program   *Smile program Taxi*

(a) Travelling 7 miles. Is £4 enough?
(b) Will 5 miles cost me more or less than £2.50?
(c) Will £5 get me to a town 9 miles away?

Shopping

 CAL programs   *Gestalt Money and Shopping*

(a) To buy 4 packs of materials costing £3.30 each. Will £10 be enough?
(b) Should I buy from a catalogue a shirt costing £1.99 for 12 weeks or buy direct for £21?
    Which is cheaper?

The list is endless. With much work done on this very important aspect of maths, students will improve their confidence as well as lose the fear of abandoning the 'exact' number, and work happily with easy numbers.

The calculator

A calculator

- allows students to reach solutions
- promotes mathematical discussion
- requires the early development of estimating and approximating skills
- eases the transfer from concrete to symbolic thinking
- allows real life numbers to be used
- allows mathematical exploration
- helps to focus on the problem rather than on the computation (especially if multiplication tables are involved)
- allows concentration on methods and concepts
- takes away some of the fear of mathematics.

I have found that I have to persuade my pupils to use a calculator because many of them feel that it is 'cheating' in some way. At other times I have to suggest to pupils that it would be better to write down exactly what they intend doing on the calculator before they do it, because some pupils use the calculator, get an answer, then forget what they have done – this last point is particularly relevant to 'grasshopper' thinkers. In a recent mock examination the symbol for the calculator was crossed out, which was an indication to the student that he had to use a non-calculator method to solve that particular problem and show his workings. He put up his hand and said, 'If I am not allowed to use a calculator how can I calculate?' He was not dyscalculic but merely a dyslexic student doing what the majority of dyslexics do when translating under stressful conditions and misunderstanding the meaning indicated by a symbol, in this case the crossed out calculator.

Difficulties with calculators

- Using a calculator is not an easy task. There are different types and they often have many functions which a pupil will probably never need to use.
- A pupil requires practice in pressing the right keys on the calculator because after reading a number he needs to be able to reproduce it accurately in order to achieve a correct answer.
- Very often a pupil will read a number correctly but reverse it when putting it into the calculator.
- He may say 'multiply' but press the addition symbol on the calculator. (Sometimes writing the symbol down in a different colour encourages him to double check that he has pressed the correct button and perhaps will help to avoid this particular error.)
- The decimal point may be ignored or put in the wrong place because the comma used to divide off the thousands will be incorrectly identified as a decimal point. On a calculator the decimal point is shown at the bottom of the display panel; so if a student places his calculator at the top of his desk then the chances are he will not be able to see the decimal point.
- The pupil should be encouraged to first read the number aloud, and then check again aloud, that this is the number that is displayed on the calculator.
- In order to estimate, a pupil needs to use easy or whole numbers and therefore has to be taught to ignore numbers after the decimal point. However, at a later date he will need to correct a number to a specified number of 'significant figures' or 'decimal places', and to do this successfully, he needs to be confident with both his calculator and with decimal places.

In these days I believe it most important that pupils with specific learning difficulties in mathematics are actively encouraged to use calculators in appropriate situations. They need to be given clear guidance on the procedures needed to obtain maximum benefit from their use. A curriculum that is investigational as well as practical encourages this, allowing pupils the chance to explore new horizons. Pupils who find using a calculator difficult need the opportunity to practise until they are confident in their own expertise. One of my pupils, when shown the fraction button, said, 'Why did I waste all those years doing fractions which I still don't understand, when I could have been shown this key and spent my time doing something that would still be useful to me?'

The fraction button

- The fraction button (FB) is: $a^b/_c$
- To put ½ into the calculator
  Press 1
  Press FB
  Press 2   1 ⌐ 2
- To put in ¾
  Press 3
  Press FB
  Press 4   3 ⌐ 4
- To put 1½ into the calculator
  Press 1
  Press FB
  Press 1
  Press FB
  Press 2   1 ⌐ 1 ⌐ 2
- A display of 2 ⌐ 1 ⌐ 4 gives an answer of 2¼.

Time

This topic poses a serious problem for many pupils, for not only do they have to know 12 hour time and 24 hour time, but they also have to recognise both digital and analogue times. They have difficulty with organisation of their own time because dates on paper can be meaningless. Often they do not know the sequence of months, so seasons and passage of time are confusing for them. Asking a pupil to say when the next bus will arrive from a certain place can be disastrous. However, I hasten to add that many timetables are often difficult to understand, especially when considering all the abbreviations that put limitations on each bus (e.g. s.o./Sunday only).

Many exercises in mathematics ask pupils to say how long a television programme lasts by looking at a television programme in the paper. They have to first read through to identify the programme, check the time it begins then find the time it ends. If a pupil is having difficulty with time this exercise can be a nightmare.

 CAL programs   *Clockwise, Gestalt Time* (see list of software)

Passage of time

Egg-timers and home-made pendulums are useful for comparing the time taken to do various activities. The use of stopwatches can be more meaningful to older students who come across them, often on the sports field.

- Try counting seconds to see how accurate a student is in estimation of time.
- Make a pendulum with a weight tied on to a piece of string and estimate the time taken for it to swing backwards and forwards.
- Egg-timers measuring different times can be used to measure the amount of time taken to walk across a room, count in twos up to fifty or count down in tens from a hundred.

1. Give pupils an index card showing months, abbreviations, plus number names as shown in Figure 5.6.

Number	Month	
1	January	– Jan
2	February	– Feb
3	March	– Mar
4	April	– Apr
5	May	– May
6	June	– Jun
7	July	– Jul
8	August	– Aug
9	September	– Sep
10	October	– Oct
11	November	– Nov
12	December	– Dec

1	one	11	eleven	30	thirty
2	two	12	twelve	40	forty
3	three	13	thirteen	50	fifty
4	four	14	fourteen	60	sixty
5	five	15	fifteen	70	seventy
6	six	16	sixteen	80	eighty
7	seven	17	seventeen	90	ninety
8	eight	18	eighteen	100	hundred
9	nine	19	nineteen	1000	thousand
10	ten	20	twenty	1000000	million

Figure 5.6: Index card showing months and number names

Words to know with respect to time. These may be written on charts and put onto the wall. At a later date the student can write them into his book and onto an alphabet card for future reference.

annual	annually	–	once a year
month	monthly	–	12 times a year
quarter	quarterly	–	4 times a year
day	daily	–	every day
week	weekly	–	every week (52)

first	1st	seventh	7th
second	2nd	eighth	8th
third	3rd	ninth	9th
fourth	4th	tenth	10th
fifth	5th	eleventh	11th
sixth	6th	twelfth	12th

last, middle, after, before, past
morning – a.m.
afternoon, evening, night – p.m.
lunch time, noon, midnight
departs, arrives, destination

hour = hr   minutes = min.   a.m. = morning   p.m. = afternoon and night

2. Teach pupils the number of days in months by putting two hands together and looking at their knuckles.
   - Starting with the left hand the knuckles are January, March, May, July.
   - Now looking at the right hand the knuckles are August, October and December. These seven months have 31 days.

Using the whole year calendar (Figure 5.9) answer the following questions.
(a) The first (1st)/second (2nd)/fifth (5th), etc., month of the year is.....................?
(b) How many months are there in the year?
(c) On what day is Christmas Day?
(d) My birthday is on.....................

Telling the time

Digital time

As children today use videos, and have digital watches they are more accustomed to digital time so I will begin with this. A great deal of work is done orally before anything is written down. Clocks that have digital displays are useful, especially if they have a clock face with movable hands which can be used later.

1. Cards with digital time written on them with the words on the reverse side are helpful to pupils; for example:

Front	Reverse
11.22	22 minutes past 11
14.26	26 minutes past 14
18.56	56 minutes past 18

This is only using past times

2. Discuss how to change 12 hour time to 24 hour time. Some pupils like to add on 12 but others prefer to add on 10 then 2.

6.51 + 12 → 18

or

6.51 + 10 → 16.51 + 2 → 18.51.

To reverse the procedure

18.51 – 12 → 6.51

or

18.51 – 10 → 8.51 – 2 → 6.51.

Some rules to write down
Changing 12 hour time to 24 hour time.

1. Any a.m. time up to 9.59 always begins with a 0. For example:

a.m. and p.m. times		24 hour time
1.25	is	0125
3.45 a.m.	is	0345
8.57 a.m.	is	0857

2. 10, 11 and 12 noon are just the same in 12 and 24 hour time. Therefore:

1015 → 1015
1108 → 1108
1238 → 1238

3. For p.m. times always add 12 to the *first two numbers*. For example:

    2.00 p.m.   →   1400 in 24 hour time
    6.30 p.m.   →   1830 in 24 hour time

A common error is to add 12 to the last two numbers so that 6.30 p.m. becomes 0642 in 24 hour time. This often happens, so be on the lookout: the problem can then be avoided.

Table 5.1, which links up analogue with 12 hour and 24 hour clock times, is useful. Students can use separate colours to identify different parts of the day or even do little drawings to remind themselves of what they do at a particular time, e.g. 8.00 a.m. eat breakfast. The table (Table 5.1) can also be copied, cut out and stuck on to a large cardboard tube so that 1.00 a.m. is next to 12.00 midnight – then students can see as they turn the tube that day is following night.

Table 5.1: Analogue times, and 12 hour and 24 hour clock times

🕐	one o'clock	1.00 a.m.	0100	morning
🕑	two o'clock	2.00 a.m.	0200	morning
🕒	three o'clock	3.00 a.m.	0300	morning
🕓	four o'clock	4.00 a.m.	0400	morning
🕔	five o'clock	5.00 a.m.	0500	morning
🕕	six o'clock	6.00 a.m.	0600	morning
🕖	seven o'clock	7.00 a.m.	0700	morning
🕗	eight o'clock	8.00 a.m.	0800	morning
🕘	nine o'clock	9.00 a.m.	0900	morning
🕙	ten o'clock	10.00 a.m.	1000	morning
🕚	eleven o'clock	11.00 a.m.	1100	morning
🕛	twelve o'clock	12.00 noon	1200	morning
🕐	one o'clock	1.00 p.m.	1300	afternoon
🕑	two o'clock	2.00 p.m.	1400	afternoon
🕒	three o'clock	3.00 p.m.	1500	afternoon
🕓	four o'clock	4.00 p.m.	1600	afternoon
🕔	five o'clock	5.00 p.m.	1700	afternoon
🕕	six o'clock	6.00 p.m.	1800	evening
🕖	seven o'clock	7.00 p.m.	1900	evening
🕗	eight o'clock	8.00 p.m.	2000	evening
🕘	nine o'clock	9.00 p.m.	2100	night
🕙	ten o'clock	10.00 p.m.	2200	night
🕚	eleven o'clock	11.00 p.m.	2300	night
🕛	twelve o'clock	12.00 midnight	0000	night

Analogue time

There are excellent teaching clocks available showing 12 hour time, 24 hour time, minutes, Roman numerals. I show pupils that it is the small hand which points to the hour – perhaps by drawing a clock and colouring in the hand. We discuss the long hand and count around in fives. Initially I try to avoid any 'to' times and use only 'past' times (see Figure 5.10). A clock face rubber stamp enables lots of practice to take place.

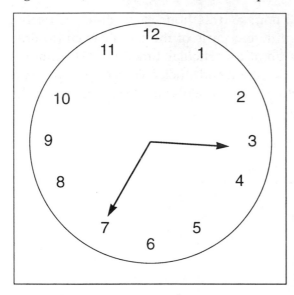

Figure 5.10: Clock face. This would be read as 35 minutes past three

The 'half past' needs to be introduced fairly quickly but I try to connect as much as possible with the digital times with which my students are familiar. Drawing a clock face, putting in the numerals and colouring half the clock can help to show half an hour.

Exercises in reading words, translating to digital time and then to analogue time are useful:

20 minutes past 8	8.20
45 minutes past 10	1045.

This exercise can be used, with a further step added, when 24 hour time is involved, for example:

2020   8.20   twenty minutes past 8.

When a student begins to master time, then more complicated times can be introduced. Students with confidence in this topic seem to grasp quarter past, twenty-five to, quarter to, if it is taught later, rather than pushing too much information at them too soon. Written problems do present more difficulties as initially the words have to be read, understood and then related to clock faces and digital time.

The fact that 60 minutes make an hour causes further problems and the calculator procedure to do time calculations is rather complicated. It is important for a tutor to remember that a dyslexic will probably be using a different strategy to read a clock. An adult dyslexic recently informed me that the first time a clock made sense to her was when her mother moved a mirror onto a wall opposite their clock. 'When Mum said that it was four o'clock, I heard the clock strike four and at the same time I saw the mirror image of the clock. Suddenly it all made sense! So, that was what they meant by four o'clock. After that I could tell the time because I related it to the mirror image of the clock.'

EGLWYSBACH – LLANDUDNO — Crosville Cymru 25

Llun i Sadwrn | Monday to Saturday

	28												
WEST SHORE	—	—											
LLANDUDNO Saf/Stp A	—	—	0900	0950	1100	1210	1300	1410	1500	1610	1700	1810	1915
Craig y Don	—	—	0905	0955	1105	1215	1305	1415	1505	1615	1705	1815	1920
Coleg Llandrillo	—	—	—	—	—	—	—	—	—	—	1710	—	—
Llanrhos	—	—	0907	0957	1107	1217	1307	1417	1507	1617	—	1817	1922
Cyff/Junc Mari Drive	—	—	0910	1000	1110	1220	1310	1420	1510	1620	—	1820	1925
Depo	0708	0740	—	—	—	—	—	—	—	—	—	—	—
A470/A55	0713	0745	0915	1005	1115	1225	1315	1425	1515	1625	1720	1825	1930
Glan Conwy Church St	—	—	—	—	—	1228	—	1428	—	1628	1723	1828	1933
Maes Hyfryd	—	—	—	—	—	1230	—	1430	—	1630	1725	1830	1935
GLAN CONWY VALE	0716	0747	0918	1008	1118		1318		1518		1726	1831	1936
Fforddias	0719	0750	0921	1011	1121		1321		1521		1729	1834	1939
Bodnant Garden	—	0754	0925	1015	1125		1325		1525		1733	1838	
EGLWYSBACH Bee	—	0759	0930	1020	1130		1330		1530		1738		
Eglwysbach (Hen Efail)	—	0800											

Look at different sorts of timetables so that a pupil may quickly find a variety of information. It is essential to point out that in bus timetables:

- each column is giving information about a different bus
- gaps mean the bus does not stop at that place
- the first time means that is when the bus starts
- the last time in the column is when it arrives at its destination.

Difficulties with measuring time

Time is usually given in hours, so it is necessary to convert minutes into fractions. To change minutes into fractions of an hour divide by 60.

30 minutes $=$ $\frac{1}{2}$ hour $=$ 0.5

15 minutes $=$ $\frac{1}{4}$ hour $=$ 0.25

45 minutes $=$ $\frac{3}{4}$ hour $=$ 0.75

5 minutes $=$ $\frac{1}{12}$ hour $=$ 0.08

20 minutes $=$ $\frac{20}{60}$ hour $=$ 0.3

Time/distance graphs

Words and symbols to know are: Speed (S), Time (T) and Distance (D). Average speed (S) is measured in either:

miles per hour   abbreviated to   mph

or

kilometres per hour   abbreviated to   km/h

Pupils need to be shown exactly what graphs are as they cannot easily interpret them because there are so many facts to be taken into consideration. On a time/distance graph

- What do the axes represent?
- What is the scale?
- How is the time shown?

Is it in 12 or 24 hour time?
What does a half represent?
What does a horizontal line on the actual graph mean?

Formulae

Distance = Speed × Time

D = S × T

$S = \dfrac{D}{T}$ $T = \dfrac{D}{S}$

$D = S \times T$

$S = \dfrac{D}{T}$

$T = \dfrac{D}{S}$

The triangles are a most useful visual memory jogger which can be put on walls. Colour helps to sort out these relationships, as does making cards with the formulae written on them. Big sheets with the letters stuck on them, perhaps made out of paper which has a rough surface, is another multi-sensory way of reinforcing this concept.

For example, a driver can only drive for two and a half hours without stopping for a break. How far can he go on a motorway at 52 mph?

T = 2.5   S = 52
D = S   × T
D = 52 × 2.5
D = 130 miles

While the need to acquire basic number skills cannot be emphasised enough, it is important to remember what is said in the following two quotations. Crombie (1992) says that:

What we must protect against is holding the child back too long because he has not mastered a certain task ... better to find a strategy to circumvent the problem, in order that a child can continue to progress with his group.

Vygotsky in Feuerstein's *Revolution in the Teaching of Intelligence* (Sharron 1987) states:

Education must be orientated not towards the yesterday of child development but towards its tomorrow.

PART 2

Teaching strategies

Chapter 6

A guide to number

Introducing a new topic

The following guidance and suggestions will assist both teacher and student when a new topic is being introduced in mathematics.

- Make it exciting and enjoyable.
- Talk about the topic; make it challenging; be interested in your students' views.
- If a student uses coloured filters or lenses, encourage him to continue to use them in mathematics.
- Read and discuss the new topic; write down words which the students may meet.
- Allow students to speculate, hypothesise, search in other directions and make connections to other topics and subject areas.
- Encourage originality in discussions among students and with the teacher.
- After reading through a problem, highlight or underline (whatever method your pupil prefers) the important parts, just as you would do in a comprehension exercise, so that instead of the pupil seeing a mass of words, certain sections become clearer and offer a 'way through' a problem.
- Once a problem has been discussed and a method decided upon, encourage the student to *write down* the mathematical symbol in the place where he normally uses it and highlight it. Ask 'Is your answer going to be bigger than the original number, or less?'

  - If the answer is going to be *bigger*, decide whether + or × is the symbol to use (+ is a slower way of doing ×).
  - If the answer is going to be *smaller*, decide whether − or ÷ is the symbol to use.

    (Dyslexic students try to avoid both of these processes!) However, the decision between − and ÷ is usually easy, as students seem to recognise the subtraction computation quickly – perhaps seeing it as the 'easy' alternative to dividing.

- If a student is confident, encourage him to estimate an answer. If the student is terrified of estimation (many of them are), do a little together to show how easy it is to use whole or easy numbers. Write the estimated answer down and then check his answers on a calculator.
- Begin to work through a problem, use pictures or diagrams only if the student finds that this method helps. Many students have said that they find drawings distract their minds from the mathematics. Encourage them to see the problem in their 'mind's eye'.

Organisational hints

- Explain why students should begin their work at the top of the page on the left hand side.
- Use books with 0.7 cm squares. This is just the right size for both numbers and letters. If 1 cm squares are needed use 1 cm squared paper, cut out the shape and stick it into the maths book. This makes the procedure very multi-sensory.
- Draw a margin down the left hand side for the actual number of the calculation and put a ring around it to divide it completely from the main computation.
- When doing long division draw a margin on the right side of the page to keep each piece of working out in the same part of the page.
- Encourage the use of rulers to keep work tidy.
- Encourage students to keep pencils, pencil sharpeners, pens and rubbers together for easy access.

Tips for basic computation

Written computation should not be undertaken by dyslexic students until they have worked with apparatus, talked a great deal about procedures and understood the concepts indicated by the four basic symbols in mathematics. Cockcroft (1982) emphasised this:

> A premature start on formal written arithmetic is likely to delay progress rather than hasten it.

Addition, subtraction and multiplication are all done from right to left, so teachers and students need to decide on a symbol which could show a student just where to begin. It could be a star, a green traffic light or simply an arrow indicating the direction of the calculation. Students need to be urged to make sure their figures are in the proper columns before they start the computation. The symbol they are using has to be highlighted so they will remember exactly which type of calculations they are doing. The carrying figure needs to be discussed, possibly with the class teacher, so that every one is using the same type of notation and position to avoid confusion later.

It is good practice to look at errors which students are making and ask them to explain exactly the procedure they are carrying out. In this way it is possible for a teacher to spot just where a student is going wrong.

A word of warning! If a student is reaching correct answers, but using a long, tedious method, please do not tell him that he needs to change, for then he may lose all confidence in his own ability and give up. I find it better, as I gradually go through other lessons, to show in small stages an easier way through to reach the same solution. Sometimes after weeks of trying to help a student to solve a problem, he will say that he has decided to abandon his long method for something more simple.

Addition with magic squares

The idea of a magic square seems to have come from China. One was found on a document called 'Lo-Shu', dated 2200 BC. In India and Tibet the magic square is a charm. A magic square is one in which the numbers, whether added upwards, downwards, across or diagonally, give the same answer, called the total.

1. Figure 6.1 shows a square partially completed, using only the numbers 4, 5 and 6. The total is 15. Can you finish the square?
2. What is the total of the magic square in Figure 6.2? Complete the square using numbers 1, 2, 3, 7, 8, and 9 once only.
3. Try to complete the magic square in Figure 6.3 (use a calculator if you wish). First find the total. (Clue – add the diagonal numbers.)

4	6	5
6	5	4
	4	6

		4
	5	
6		

15		13
	12	
11		

Figure 6.1: Square (partially completed)

Figure 6.2: Complete the square

Figure 6.3: Complete the magic square

Factors

Numbers which divide exactly into another number without a remainder are factors. A factor 'creature' can help, especially if separate cards showing all the factors of one number are made using coloured sticky paper to make the creature exciting. Creatures with lots of legs enable students to write the relating factors on separate legs.

The 'Factorpus' (Figure 6.4) can help to make the concept of factors 'stick'. For example, complete the Factorpus of 12, writing the factors on the ends of the legs as shown:

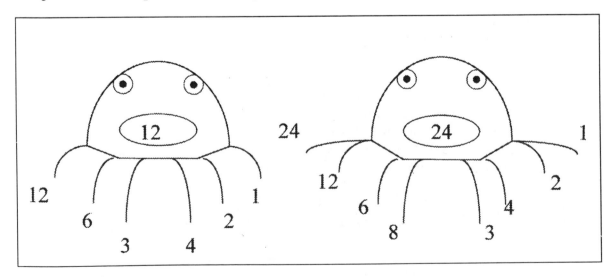

Figure 6.4: Factorpus

- start with 1 1×12
- then try 2 2×6
- then try 3 3×4

We go on like this until we find a repeated number; for example, complete the Factorpus of 24:

- start with 1 1×24
- then try 2 2×12
- then try 3 3×8
- then try 4 4×6

A table square can be useful in helping students to find factors as well as number facts as they search through the square to find answers. Once a student has made a pack of factor cards, games can be played to show how quick and accurate he has become.

Some hints for finding factors

- 2 is a factor of all even numbers
- 3 is a factor when the digits of a number add up to 3, 6 or 9
- 5 is a factor if a number ends in 5 or 0
- 9 is a factor if the digits add up to 9

A calculator can be used to see if a number is a factor. For example, is 9 a factor of 151?

- Enter 151 on the calculator
- Divide it by 9 and press the equals sign
- The answer is 16.7777.

This shows that 9 is not a factor of 151. If the answer had been a number without a decimal point, the number would have been a factor. For example, is 8 a factor of 256?

- Enter 256
- Divide by 8 and press the equals sign
- The answer is 32, this a whole number. 8 is a factor of 256.

Multiples

This is another word which dyslexics find difficult to understand. It identifies a group of numbers. Once again with the help of a table square we can discuss the word using easy numbers. For example,

     4   Is 4 a multiple of 2?
     4 is in the 2 times table so it is a multiple of 2.

Once students realise that multiples are the numbers in the times tables, there is no problem.

Prime numbers

A prime number is any integer which has only itself and 1 as a factor.

1 is not prime.

- 2, 3, 5, 7, 11, 13, 17, 19 are important prime numbers up to 20. Colour them on a number square. Make index cards of them and put them in a prominent place for students to see all the time.
- Using practical apparatus (e.g. centicubes, multilink) show that the prime numbers can only be put into groups of ones and themselves. They cannot be put into groups of twos, threes, fours, etc. Do this practically.
- Allow students to colour in the prime numbers on a 1–100 number square.

Odd and even numbers

1. Encourage discussion about odd and even numbers. Try to make up rhymes that could help. For example,

   Try to remember the following thought
   Even numbers end 2, 4, 6, 8 or nought.
   Remember, remember the following rhyme
   Odd numbers end 1, 3, 5, 7 or nine.

2. Point out that the last digit dictates whether a number is odd or even:

57	the 7 makes the number odd
132	the 2 makes the number even
17,846	the 6 makes the number even.

3. Colouring in patterns and constant referral to odd and even number patterns on a 1–100 square helps reinforce these number facts.

Directed numbers (positive and negative numbers)

Negative numbers are shown in mathematics with a – sign placed on the left of the number (–3 is read as minus 3 and means negative 3).

Negative numbers are less than 0.

Make a number line on cardboard to show both positive and negative numbers (Figure 6.5). Use colour to separate the positive side from the negative side. Put a drawing pin through the zero and turn the card through ninety degrees in an anti-clockwise direction. Students can then see that the scale is the same whether vertical or horizontal. Making temperature scales and reading thermometers are starting points to assist students with this concept.

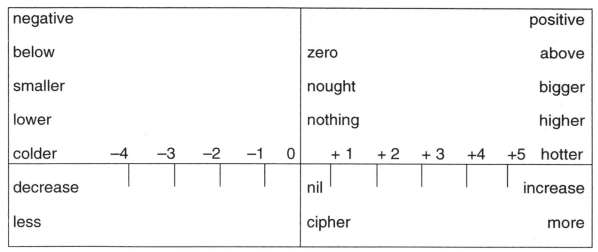

Figure 6.5: Number line on cardboard

1. Put the following temperatures in order starting with the lowest:

   –3°C, –9°C, –1°C, 1°C, 6°C, –4°C.

2. Fill the following gaps with the word 'colder' or 'warmer'.
   4°C is ....than 6°C
   0°C is ....than –3°C
   –1°C is ....than 1°C
   –6°C is ....than –7°C
   0°C is ....than –5°C

Multiplying and dividing negative numbers

Students are often confused when they have to calculate with negative signs in algebra. The following simple tips may help.

- If removing a bracket, *beware* a *minus* sign outside a bracket. It changes every sign inside the bracket. For example:

  –3(b + 2)   becomes   –3b – 6
  –a(6 – c)   becomes   –6c + ac

- When multiplying negative numbers always remember that:

  minus   ×   minus   =   plus
  plus   ×   plus   =   plus
  minus   ×   plus   =   minus
  plus   ×   minus   =   minus

  This also applies to divide:

  minus   ÷   minus   =   plus
  plus   ÷   plus   =   plus
  minus   ÷   plus   =   minus
  plus   ÷   minus   =   minus

Agnew *et al.* (1996) help with the following mnemonics:

Signs the same, play the game: make it PLUS
Signs are different, not the same: make it MINUS

CAL programs   *Circus, Ten out of Ten Geometry, Ten out of Ten Algebra* (see list of software)

Students can make a table square showing all four quadrants (see Figure 6.6) which may help when students begin to work with coordinates and other related topics.

-25	-20	-15	-10	-5		5	10	15	20	25
-20	-16	-12	-8	-4		4	8	12	16	20
-15	-12	-9	-6	-3		3	6	9	12	15
-10	-8	-6	-4	-2		2	4	6	8	10
-5	-4	-3	-2	-1		1	2	3	4	5
5	4	3	2	1		-1	-2	-3	-4	-5
10	8	6	4	2		-2	-4	-6	-8	-10
15	12	9	6	3		-3	-6	-9	-12	-15
20	16	12	8	4		-4	-8	-12	-16	-20
25	20	15	10	5		-5	-10	-15	-20	-25

Figure 6.6: A table square

'Greater than' and 'less than'

Sometimes instead of the equals sign indicating a balance of equal amounts on each side, the following signs > or < are used. These signs indicate an inequality, showing that one side of the balance is bigger than the other.

The words for 'greater than' are represented by the symbol >
  'bigger than'
  'more than'
The words for 'less than'   are represented by the symbol <
  'smaller than'

The Greedy Robot is ideal for teaching students the importance of placing the symbol correctly. The robot only eats the biggest numbers and that is why his open mouth is pointing towards them. Once students become used to this the robot's body can be missed out and only the basic symbol remains.

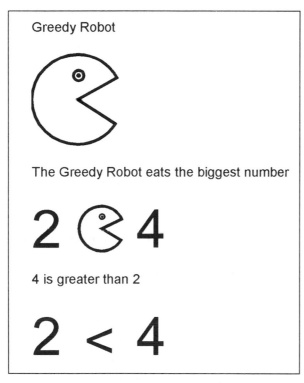

Figure 6.7: Greedy Robot

Multiplication

If a student has found satisfactory strategies for working out his times tables then, providing that he takes note of his 'starting' place, he should be able to do short multiplication calculations easily enough. However, long multiplication, without a calculator, is another matter altogether. After years of trying many methods (mostly to no avail) I have found that the Chinese Lattice method is the simplest way to help students to do it successfully, possibly because the imposed structure is so consistent or perhaps because it relies on the spatial strengths of a dyslexic student. The hardest part is doing the lattice quickly but if students are working on 0.7 cm squared paper, splitting the squares with diagonal lines still leaves a large enough space for the numbers. Some of my students like to use colour for the diagonal lines as it seems to help them to know where they are.

Chinese Lattice method

Two examples of the Chinese Lattice method are provided below.
(1)   Multiply 64 by 58
Do a quick estimation:

60	×	60	=	count the noughts is 00	put these in to the answer
6	×	6	=	36	put these in to the answer
		Answer	=	3600	

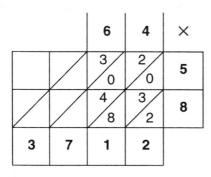

Figure 6.8: Chinese Lattice (Example 1)

Method (see Figure 6.8)

1. You can start in any square and multiply the top number by the side number, i.e.

    $4 \times 5 = 20$ $6 \times 5 = 30$ $4 \times 8 = 32$ $6 \times 8 = 48$

    noting that the tens number is written above the diagonal line and the units figure written underneath.
2. The diagonal lines can be identified as 1, 2, 3, etc., starting from the bottom right hand corner.

    - Put a piece of card across the first diagonal line and copy down the number underneath that line (in this example 2) and put in the first square.
    - Then put the card across the second diagonal line and add together the numbers underneath that line (in this example 11), so 1 is put into the second square and 1 is carried forward.
    - Then put the card across the third diagonal line and add together the numbers underneath that line (in this example 6 + 1 = 7), so 7 is put into the third square.
    - Then put the card across the fourth diagonal line and add together the numbers underneath that line (in this example 3), so 3 is put into the fourth square.
    - Answer is 3712.

(2)   Multiply 416 by 92

Do a quick estimation:

400	×	100	=	count two noughts on to the 40
		Answer	=	40000

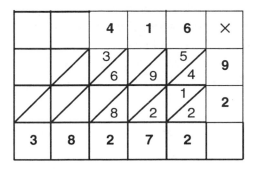

Figure 6.9: Chinese Lattice (Example 2)

Method (see Figure 6.9)

1. Multiply for each square (as shown in the following two lines)

   $6 \times 9 = 54$ $\quad$ $1 \times 9 = 9$ $\quad$ $4 \times 9 = 36$
   $6 \times 2 = 12$ $\quad$ $1 \times 2 = 2$ $\quad$ $4 \times 2 = 8$

2. Starting with the first diagonal, add up all numbers underneath and put them into the answer. Answer is 38272.

Multiplying using groups of tens

Another way which can be quite successful with students is for them to do small multiplications and then add the answers together (see example (3) below).

(3) To multiply 397 by 34
    Do a simple estimate:

   $400 \quad \times \quad 30 \quad = \quad$ count the noughts 000 $\quad$ put them in to the answer
   $ 4 \quad \times \quad 3 \quad = \quad 12 $ put 12 in to the answer
   $ \text{Answer} \quad = \quad 12000$

   Method

   $397 \quad \times \quad 10 \quad = \quad 3970$
   $397 \quad \times \quad 10 \quad = \quad 3970 \qquad + \qquad\qquad 397$
   $397 \quad \times \quad 10 \quad = \quad \underline{3970} \qquad\qquad \underline{\times \quad\quad 4}$
   $397 \quad \times \quad 30 \quad = \quad 11910 \qquad\qquad\quad 1588$
   $ + \quad \underline{1588}$
   $397 \quad \times \quad 34 \quad = \quad \underline{13498}$

Division

Division can be written in three ways:

(a) $387 \div 9$

(b) $9\,|\,387$

(c) $\dfrac{387}{9}$

Division with a calculator is complex because the student has to translate the question properly or he will reach the wrong answer.

To use a calculator in

(a) $387 \div 9$ $\quad$ the student will enter the numbers starting on the left and move towards the right entering each number and symbol as it appears.

(b) $9\overline{)387}$ The student will enter the numbers inside the division shape first (the numbers on the right), then enter the division sign and then enter the number on the left. This particular operation is carried out incorrectly so often I now have a 'Nudge' policy. If they put the wrong number in first I nudge them and because we have discussed this problem so often they automatically re-enter their numbers correctly.

(c) $\dfrac{387}{9}$

- Enter the number above the line first   387
- 'Read' the line between top and bottom numbers as divide   ÷
- Then enter the number from under the line   9
- Finally press   =

Division without a calculator

Short division without a calculator can be complicated. For example:

387 ÷ 9

- Translate the division sign ÷ into (as from (a) to (b))
- $9\overline{)387}$
- Starting from the left:

How many nines in 3? = none   carry the three forward = 38
How many nines in 38? = 4   write this on top over the 8
2 left over   carry the two forward = 27
How many nines in 27? = 3   write this on top over the 7
    Answer is 43.

Long division

I think that of all procedures in numeracy the one that gives my students most problems is long division without a calculator. As soon as they see the calculator sign crossed out next to a division calculation, fear sets in. Sometimes the anxiety it produces can hinder a student's progress and achievement through the rest of the paper. I usually tell them in an examination to do that question last, to put all thoughts of division without a calculator out of their heads and to concentrate on another topic which they can do successfully to ease their worries.

However, I do try to work out strategies to help. The one with which I have had most success is the following. When I showed this method to a solicitor friend of mine she said, 'That is the first time I have ever understood what long division meant. In school I went through the motions but hadn't got the faintest idea what they were talking about!'

Divide 1118.6 by 17
Estimation: 1000 ÷ 20
                       cross off a nought in both numbers
                       100 ÷ 2
                       Answer = 50
Rewrite the calculation as shown in Figure 6.10.

```
      0   0   6   5  .  8
1  7 | 1   1   1   8  .  6
```

write these	1	17
numbers in	2	34
colour	3	51
	4	68
	5	85
	6	102
	7	119
	8	136
	9	153

Figure 6.10 Long division without a calculator

Method

1. Set out the calculation.
2. Write out the numbers one to nine in a colour, e.g. red, in the right hand margin.
3. Write out the 17 times table.
   Do this by adding 17 to the previous number in your head
   or put 17 on the calculator, press the + key twice, followed by the = key and 17 will be added on each time, continue pressing the = key to add on 17s.
4. Put a decimal point into the answer directly above the decimal point in the question.
5. Work as follows:

   - How many 17s are there in 1   = 0 Carry the 1 to the right to make 11
   - How many 17s are there in 11   = 0 Carry the 11 to the right to make 111
   - How many 17s are there in 111 = **6** and 9 left over
                                            Carry the 9 to the right to make 98
   - How many 17s are there in 98   = **5** and 13 left over
                                              Carry the 13 to the right to make 136
   - How many 17s are there in 136 = **8**

The answer is 65.8 (which could be written in red to match the numbers down the side). I have not found a better alternative for doing long division.

A fun way of checking answers

Casting out nines

To cast out nines you simply add up each digit in an answer. For example:
$$567 = 5 + 6 + 7 = 18$$
$$18 = 1 + 8 = 9 \quad \text{(we will call 9 our 'magic answer')}$$
If a calculation is correct:

the magic numbers of both the calculation and the answer will be the same

To check the answer we got for the first example (1) under the heading *Chinese Lattice method* (see page 62):

```
        64   ×      58   =   3712
6      + 4   ×     5 + 8  =   3 + 7 + 1 + 2
10     ×    13           =   13
1 + 0  ×    1 + 3        =   1 + 3
1      ×    4            =   4
            4            =   4   (the magic numbers are the same)
```

To check the answer we got for the example in *Multiplying using groups of tens* (see page 63):

```
397      ×    34              =   13498
3 + 9 + 7  ×    3 + 4          =   1 + 3 + 4 + 9 + 8
19       ×    7               =   25
1 + 9    ×    7               =   2 + 5
10       ×    7               =   7
1             ×    7          =   7
              7              =   7   (the magic numbers are the same)
```

To check the answer we got for the example of long division (see page 65).

```
1118.6              ÷     17     =   65.8
1 + 1 + 1 + 8 + 6   ÷     1 + 7  =   6 + 5 + 8
17                  ÷     8      =   19
1 + 7               ÷     8      =   1 + 9
8                   ÷     8      =   10
                          1      =   1 + 0
                          1      =   1   (the magic numbers are the same)
```

Students can be helped by:

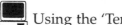 Using the 'Tenners' program (*Smile Mathematics*, see section listing software)

- using Arrow cards
- playing the 'Place Value' game (Taskmaster, see Resources section for address)
- talking about the problem, using colour to make hundreds, tens and units look different
- lots of practice – encouraged in a friendly way.

Rounding off

We are often required to read numbers which give an approximate size as opposed to an exact size. We can do this by rounding off a number to a specific size and a number line may be useful to do this.

- Round off 2718 to the nearest 10
  2718 is nearer to 2720 than to 2710   Answer = 2720 (see Figure 6.11)

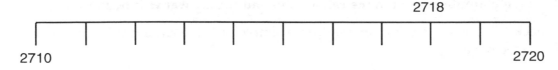

Figure 6.11: Number line (nearest 10)

- Round off 2718 to the nearest 100

  2718 is nearer to 2700 than to 2800   Answer is 2700 (see Figure 6.12)

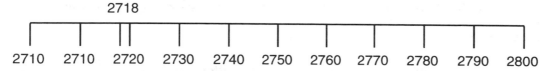

Figure 6.12: Number line (nearest 100)

- Round off 2718 to the nearest 1000

  2718 is nearer to 3000 than to 2000   Answer is 3000 (see Figure 6.13)

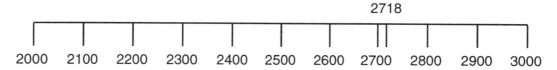

Figure 6.13: Number line (nearest 1000)

Exercises using a money number line.

- Round off the following amounts to the nearest 10p (refer to Figure 6.14)

Figure 6.14: Number line (nearest 10p)

(a) 18p   (e) £1.18
(b) 69p   (f) £2.69
(c) 32p   (g) £3.32
(d) 82p   (h) £5.82

- Round off the following to the nearest £1 (refer to Figure 6.15)

(a) 87p   (d) £5.60
(b) £2.29   (e) £8.68
(c) £3.42   (f) £9.19

Figure 6.15: Number line (nearest £1)

- Round off the following to the nearest £100 (refer to Figure 6.16)

(a) £497.00   (d) £526.33
(b) £185.11   (e) £322.10
(c) £640.13   (f) £876.50

Figure 6.16: Number line (nearest £100)

An interesting description of a number line written by Mark Scult, a mathematics teacher, was taken from the Internet recently.

I have always had a very strong mental image of a number line, right from primary school days when I first started to get to grips with maths (not my favourite subject in those days). Mine is a full blown three dimensional number line that could be modelled out of a stiffened tape measure to hang in space ... The trouble is nobody else seems to know what I am talking about if I mention it. So I thought I would mention it here as some dyslexics do have powerful visualisation abilities.

Correcting to specific numbers of decimal places

Another way of giving an approximate number is by reading it to a specific number of decimal places.

Write down the abbreviations:

     correct – corr   decimal places – dec. pl. or d.p.

To correct a number to 2 decimal places emphasise:

- Only the numbers after the decimal point are involved.
- The numbers before the decimal point stay the same.

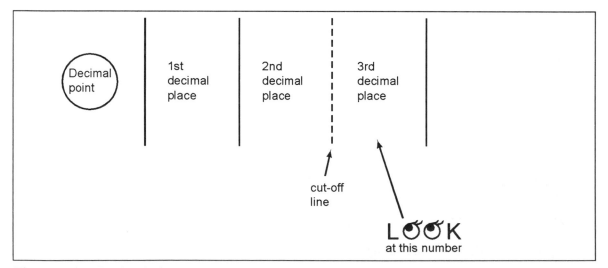

Figure 6.17: Decimal places

Procedure to correct a number to 2 d.p. (refer to Figure 6.17)

    1. Count two numbers after the decimal point and draw in a cut-off line.
    2. Look at the number to the right of the cut-off line (look right!).

3. If it is 5 or more, add 1 to the number on the left of the cut-off line (look left!); for example,
   correct 26.368 to 2 d.p.

       +1

   e.g. 26.36 | 8
   Answer is 26.37
4. If the number is less than 5 then simply write the number with two digits after the decimal point; for example,
   correct 26.364 to 2 d.p.
   26.36 | 4   Answer is 26.36

Significant figures

Another way to read numbers to an approximate size is by giving them correct to a specific number of significant figures. To 'correct' a number to a particular number of significant figures emphasises:

- Noughts at the beginning of a number can be ignored.
- Nought inside a number must not be ignored.
- Every other digit in the number must not be ignored.

The procedure is the same as for correcting a number to a specific number of decimal places.

Fractions

A very high percentage of the dyslexic (and non-dyslexic) students that I have taught feel threatened by fractions. 'I've never understood them!' is the usual statement if we decide to review them. Students are introduced to fractions very early in their education but still find them a mystery when they are older. Hart (1981) stated '... there may be a case for postponement of all work involving fractions until the secondary school stage. Partly re-teaching ... causes frustration and boredom on the part of the learner.'

In life we do very little with fractions apart from a half or a quarter. It is only for certain careers that students will need to use fractions and then the mathematics will be quite specifically taught by specialists within that field. However students do have to deal with fractions in the mathematics syllabus and the following are methods or equipment that I have used to help students.

Words to know

cut	divide	split	equal	same	share
half	halves	quarter	third	whole	

Methods

1. Using A4 paper
   - Fold and cut up the paper to show $\frac{1}{2}$s

Colour them in and write $^1/_2$ and 'a half'

Stick them together again to show that two halves make a whole sheet of A4

Discuss 2/2 = 1 (whole).

- Use the same method to show $^1/_4$s (quarters, fourths), and $^1/_3$ (thirds), making sure at the end of the lesson the student understands that 4/4 = 1 and 3/3 = 1.

2. Using pieces of string 24 cm long
   - Fold and cut into halves
   - Fold and cut into quarters
   - Fold and cut into thirds.

3. Using bars of chocolate or biscuits

   These can be divided up and broken, as was done with the A4 paper and the string, but the end results can be eaten and sometimes students remember the eating part long after the cutting and sticking has gone!

   (I taught two boys who used to come to my house for lessons every week. Each week they had Vimto and biscuits before the lessons started. They are now 21 years old and if I see either of them they always talk with great fondness of their lessons with me and how they remember the Vimto and biscuits which we often linked to fractions in problems!)

4. Using 12 coloured marbles in a bag
   - Ask the student to give you half of them. How many in a half?
   - Do the same with a quarter and a third.

   If a student is doing this correctly then possibly you could record what you have done and ask him to check it to see if he agrees. Use other numbers of marbles, too.

5. Using a calculator
   - To find a half, divide by 2
   - To find a quarter, divide by 4
   - To find a third, divide by 3.

   Allow students the opportunity to try this out to see just how easy it is. For example, Find a half of 156 ($^1/_2 \times$ 156 or 156 ÷ 2)   Enter 156 and divide by 2 = 78

   Using the Fraction Button (FB) find a half of 156

      enter 1, press FB

      enter 2

      press X

      enter 156

      press = 78.

6. CAL program   *Wall and Tower from the Smile Mathematics program* (see section listing software).
   - Fraction strips can be purchased from Taskmaster (see Resources section).

Students can place the fraction strips in front of the computer and build a fraction wall with the strips while they are building up the Fraction Wall on the computer screen. Once they have completed the Wall on the computer, allow a student the time to draw his own fraction wall in his book, colouring in the different fractions with different colours. In this way the student is able to see the connection between the different fractions. When he has become more confident with fractions he could try the 'Tower' program from the Smile program.

1 whole						
1 half			1 half			
1 third		1 third		1 third		
1 quarter		1 quarter		1 quarter		1 quarter
1 sixth	1 sixth	1 sixth	1 sixth	1 sixth	1 sixth

Figure 6.18: Fraction wall

7. Using the calculator for more complex questions

Example (a) Find $^3/_4$ of £20.00   (*Remember* 'of ' means ✕)
Press in order   3   FB   4   ✕   20 = 15

Example (b) The favourite drink for one third of the class is Coke, for one quarter it is Lemonade, for one eighth it is Lilt. The rest prefer water. What fraction of the class prefer water?

$$(^1/_3 + ^1/_4 + ^1/_8 = {^{17}/_{24}})$$

Press in order 1   FB   3   +
                1   FB   4   +
                1   FB   8   =   17/24

If 17/24 do not prefer water and 24/24 represents the whole class
Then 7/24 is the fraction that prefer water.

Index cards to file under fraction need to be numbered, each one showing a different type of question with an example written clearly on the card. 'FB' should always be written in the same colour to give consistency and early identification. Other aspects such as the line dividing the top of the fraction from the bottom could be drawn in another colour. As students progress through the National Curriculum they will hopefully become more confident with using fractions, as constant referrals are made to them.

'Trystan's strategy'
Trystan, a student aged 13, was faced with the following question on fractions:

'Is 4/3 bigger than one whole?'

He said that a 1/4 was 15 but he was not sure about a third. I questioned him further about these numbers and discovered that for him a whole one was always 60. We discussed that to find a third of something you divide by three. He quickly calculated that a third of 60 was 20, therefore 4/3 were 80. He then saw clearly that 80 was bigger than 60. His answer to the original question was 'Yes, 4/3 was bigger than one whole'. Trystan had developed his own personal strategy to deal with fractions by basing the whole concept around the number 60. This example shows that a dyslexic student is able to develop his own internal logic which could have the same validity in terms of arriving at the correct solution, as the accepted objective mode of logical thinking in mathematics.

Percentages

To find a percentage

per cent means out of a hundred

decrease means less (subtract)   increase means more (add)

% looks like a divide if slightly altered   **/00 looks like a hundred**

To find a percentage of something we divide by 100 somewhere in the calculation.

Some useful facts that my pupils use

50%	=	$\frac{1}{2}$	=	÷	by	2		
25%	=	$\frac{1}{4}$	=	÷	by	4		
75%	=	$\frac{3}{4}$	=	÷	by	4	× by	3
10%	=	$\frac{1}{10}$	=	÷	by	10		
20%	=	$\frac{2}{10}$	=	÷	by	10	× by	2
30%	=	$\frac{3}{10}$	=	÷	by	10	× by	3
40%	=	$\frac{4}{10}$	=	÷	by	10	× by	4
60%	=	$\frac{6}{10}$	=	÷	by	10	× by	6
70%	=	$\frac{7}{10}$	=	÷	by	10	× by	7
80%	=	$\frac{8}{10}$	=	÷	by	10	× by	8
90%	=	$\frac{9}{10}$	=	÷	by	10	× by	9
5%	=	$\frac{1}{20}$	=	÷	by	20		
1%	=	$\frac{1}{100}$	=	÷	by	100		

Percentage on a calculator

The percentage button works differently on each calculator, making its usage complicated so students tend to avoid it. Some students discover that percentages can be done quickly using a decimal fraction on the calculator.

Percentages as decimal fractions

percentage		*decimal fraction*	
2%	2 divide by 100	=	0.02
8%	8 divide by 100	=	0.08
16%	16 divide by 100	=	0.16
35%	35 divide by 100	=	0.35
72%	72 divide by 100	=	0.72

The decimal fraction must always be followed by the multiplication sign (followed by ✕)

Do the 'followed by ✕' in a bright colour.

Students make a card with these values to stick up on the wall. When they need to find a percentage they remember that they can use the decimal fraction which speeds up the calculation.

Making connections

Students will usually have dealt with fractions and decimals by the time they meet percentages. A table making connections between fractions/decimal fractions/percentages can be helpful. Henderson (1989), page 49, shows this clearly in pictures.

Fraction	Method	Decimal	Method	Percentage
$\frac{1}{2}$ →	Divide the top 1 by the bottom 2	0.5 →	multiply by 100	50%
75/100	Draw a line under 75, under the line put a 1 followed by 00	0.75 ←	divide by 100	75% ←

Figure 6.19: Table making connections between fractions/decimal fractions/percentages

To change a fraction into a percentage
Question 1
These were the marks you got in the following subjects.
Which was your best subject?
Which was your worst?
Put them in order starting with 1 for the best.
Then work out the percentage to check your estimate.

English $17/25 \times 100 = 68\%$
Maths $32/40 \times 100 = 80\%$
History $27/30 \times 100 = 90\%$
Geography $41/60 \times 100 = 68\%$
Music $11/15 \times 100 = 73\%$
Art $53/70 \times 100 = 76\%$

This example relates closely to a student's own life so can be a good aid to memory especially if colour is used.

To find a percentage using money
Question 2
What is 16% of £912?
$$\frac{16}{100} \times 912$$
$0.16 \times 912 = £145.92$

Using decrease

Question 3

After one year a car which costs £16000 decreases 12% in value. What is its value in £s after one year?

$$\frac{12}{100} = 0.12$$

$$0.12 \times £16000 = £1920$$
$$16000 - £1920 = £14080$$

Fractional percentage

- Work out the actual number involved with the fraction
- Compare that to the original number
- Multiply by 100

Question 4

A bag holding 56 kg of potatoes was left in the rain. 14 kg of potatoes went bad. What was the percentage of potatoes that did not go bad?

Actual number that did not go bad is $56 - 14 = 42$
Over the original $42/56 \times 100 = 75\%$

Question 5

A dress which cost £83.50 was reduced in a sale to £48.00. What was the percentage reduction?

Actual reduction in £s is   £83.50 – £48.00 = £35.50
Over the original amount in £s $35.50/83.50 \times 100 = 43\%$

Once again putting different examples onto separate cards allows a student to file under percentage and be able to see a variety of methods that appertain to the same topic.

'Ben's strategy'

Ben, aged 17, was given the following question.

> Twenty-four students went on a school trip. The number of students in the school was 150. What percentage of students had gone on the trip?

Ben wrote down $\frac{150}{24} \times 100 = 16\%$

He had got the correct answer but the wrong calculation written down. I asked him how he had reached that answer and he told me that when he divided 150 by 24 and multiplied by 100 he got 625% which he knew was wrong. So, he inverted the fraction on his calculator and divided 24 by 150 then multiplied by 100 and got 16% which seemed to be right. I asked if he did this often and he replied in the affirmative, adding that he often became confused when he checked through his paper because what was written down was not always the method he had used to find an answer.

Money and shopping

As mentioned earlier, students need to practise giving and receiving change from 50p, £1, £5 and £10 using either real, cardboard or plastic money. If we are shopping in real life the change we receive is usually 'added on' to the amount we have spent. However, to work out change on paper we have to do a subtraction calculation. If students, regardless of their age, are having difficulty with this, they need to practise shopping using real objects to buy. Eventually, when they have become more confident, they should be taken to the local store to do some real shopping. Although older students are constantly shopping some do not recognise the actual coins or their value.

Exercises

The following exercises are designed to reinforce understanding. (The **answers** are given in Appendix 2).

In Britain we use the following coins:

1p   2p   5p   10p   20p   50p   £1

We can write £1 in **decimal form** and this is how it looks £1.00

| £1 + 10p in **decimal form** | is | £1.10 |
| £1 + 2p   in **decimal form** | is | £1.02 |

1. Write the following amounts in **decimal form**

   (a) 50p   (b) £1 + 1p   (c) 5p   (d) £3 + 20p

2. (a) What is the total **in pence** of adding together the answers to question 1?
   (b) Write this answer in a £ **decimal form**.

3. Complete the table (Table 6.1), adding up the amounts in the horizontal columns and expressing the answer in both **pence** and **decimal form**.

Table 6.1: Adding money (pence and decimal answers)

| | | | | | | | Total | |
1p	2p	5p	10p	20p	50p	£1	Pence	Decimal
3	2	0	1	2	1	1	207	2.07
1	0	1	1	1	0	1		
2	1	3	1	2	0	0		
2	3	2	1	0	3	2		
1	4	1	2	3	2	1		
2	0	5	3	4	3	4		

4. Use only 1p, 2p, 5p, 10p, 20p, 50p and £1 coins to make the 'Total', complete the table (Table 6.2). (The first line is done for you.)

5. The £1 coin replaced the £1 note but we still have £5, £10, £20 and £50 notes (£100 notes are used in Scotland). Using all the coins, plus the notes, show how you would pay for the items in Table 6.3.

Table 6.2: Coins making 'totals'

£1	50p	20p	10p	5p	2p	1p	Total
1	1	2				1	£1.91
							27p
							63p
							£1.47
							£3.39
							£4.78
							£3.98

Table 6.3: Using notes and coins to pay for items

Item	Cost	Notes					Coins						
		£50	£20	£10	£5	£1	50p	20p	10p	5p	2p	1p
Paper	35p											
Shoes	£24.99											
Tape	£8.27											
Book	£12.76											
TV	£210.00											
Video	£12.45											

6. Complete the following:

   (a)   34p   (b)   98p   (c)   36p
          56p   13p   35p
        + 13p   + 24p   + 99p

   (d) £1.45   (e)   £2.49   (f)   £89.20
       £1.39   £3.10   £16.43
     + £5.28   + £20.38   + £22.23

7. Find the values of the following. (You may use your calculator.)
   (a) £14.20   × 6
   (b) £18.50   − £5
   (c) £249   − £126.58
   (d) £126.96 − £6

Chapter 7

A guide to algebra

Dyslexic difficulties with algebra

W. H. Cockcroft in 1982 stated: 'Algebra is ... a source of considerable confusion and negative attitudes among pupils' (DES 1982, *The Cockcroft Report*).

Many of my students ask the question, 'What is algebra for?'

I try to explain that it is a magical way of looking at patterns and finding solutions but I find that, for dyslexics, it presents great problems. The mention of 'algebra' seems to throw both students and their parents into a state of panic. The different combinations in algebra cause confusion because not only do they have to read the numbers correctly but also the letters and symbols.

The difficulties a dyslexic experiences with 'bs' and 'ds' as well as 'qs', 'ps' and '9s' show themselves throughout this topic. A hurried 4 and an untidy continental 7 can easily be confused with an A if they are put together in a question. Some years ago a student successfully decided that he could complete his GCSE examination leaving the 'algebra' questions until last and then use non-algebraic methods to find solutions. However, these days the algebra content in the examination is considerable, so students have to become fairly proficient in algebra in order to pass.

Students need to be taught the following facts *very slowly*. Tips relating to algebra are:

- a in algebra means $+1a$ x in algebra means $+1x$
- The + or − is connected to the letter or number on the right: for example,
  $2 - x$ means $+2$ and $-x$
  $a - b$ means $+a$ and $-b$
- The multiplication symbol is not used in algebra to avoid confusion with the letter x. Letters or symbols close together, brackets and indices mean *multiply*.

1. Letters or symbols put close together

$2x$	means	2 multiplied by x	$2 \times x$	$x + x$	$= 2x$
$3a$	means	3 multiplied by a	$3 \times a$	$a + a + a$	$= 3a$
$4x$	means	4 multiplied by x	$4 \times x$	$x + x + x + x =$	$4x$

2. A bracket, e.g. 3(a) means 3 multiplied by a

3. Indices also mean multiplication

- 3^2 means   3 multiplied by 3 3×3 =   9
  b^2 means   b multiplied by b
  6^3 means $6 \times 6 \times 6$ =   216
  x^3 means $x \times x \times x$

- $4x$ take away x is not 4, i.e.
  $4x - x$ = $3x$ $(x + x + x + x) - x$ = $3x$

- The equals sign = is used as a balance to show that one side of an equation is the same size as the other.

A practical approach to algebra

1. Use coloured multilink cubes of two colours, e.g. black and white, to make a pattern.

Put in the colours	white	black	white	black	white	black	white
Change to initials	w	b	w	b	w	b	w
Collect up	4w	+	3b				

Figure 7.1: Multilink pattern

2. Allow students to make up many easy different patterns, and write down their patterns in letters.

- When students are confident make more complex patterns:

Figure 7.2: Multilink, more complex pattern

	white	black	black	white	black	black	white	black	black
	w	b	b	w	b	b	w	b	b
Each pattern is		w	+	2b					
Pattern repetition is	3(w	+	2b)						

In this way students begin to see patterns, pattern repetition, practical use of brackets and also begin to pick up general algebraic expressions.

Some practical examples using multilink

The examples (Figure 7.3) are taken from an idea by William Gibb and demonstrated by Ann MacNamara (Leeds University 1993). Work out the numbers to go into the big boxes. (The **answers** to examples (1) to (8) (Figures 7.3 and 7.4) are given in Appendix 3.)

- Use the number of cubes stated above the squares.
- The numbers in the little circles show the total number of cubes that go into the big boxes on either side.

The first one is done for you (see (1)). Try to find a quick way of getting your answers. Think hard about what you are doing.

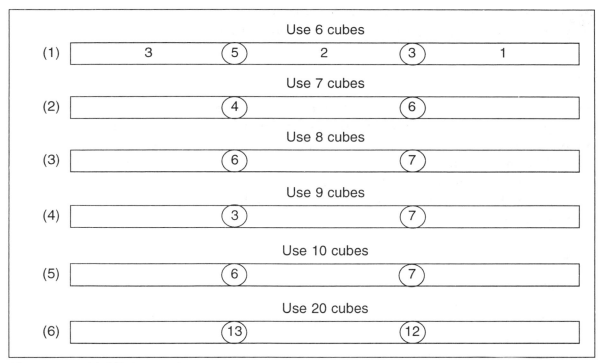

Figure 7.3: Multilink exercises

Now try the examples in Figure 7.4.
General rule: Find the number in the 'middle' box. Now write the rule.

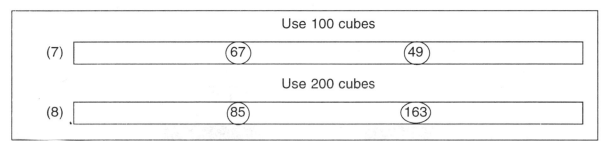

Figure 7.4: More multilink exercises

Equations

Most dyslexic students struggle with equations regardless of how many different methods they are shown. However, as stated before, they have to acquire some level of competence in order to pass their examinations. Another big problem with finding solutions to equations is that students with 'grasshopper' learning styles will do simple equations easily in their heads without writing down a single piece of working out. The 'inchworm' will quickly grasp the idea of treating each side the same which works well for simple equations. Both groups find that the method they have adopted for simple equations lets them down when they need to solve complex examples.

The only way to enable students to succeed is to repeat, revise and reinforce his own strategies over the years, using colour and practical materials (if possible), so that by the time the examination arrives a method may have gone into the long-term memory. This problem is discussed in detail in *Dyslexia and Mathematics* (Miles and Miles 1992, page 70).

CAL program *Ten out of Ten Algebra* (see list of software). Games on algebra from Taskmaster, e.g. Equation Dominoes, are helpful (see Resources section).

Investigations

Investigations into various pattern formations and connecting them up in an algebraic way is popular nowadays. I find that pupils can often spot the pattern but are unable to connect it with an algebraic formula. Many teachers have a favourite way of teaching the connection and as long as it is in slow, easy steps which the pupil understands, it is acceptable. As patterns are such an important part of mathematics, it is hoped that pupils can enjoy identifying them and so lessen their fear of this subject. The following check-list has been helpful:

Investigation check-list

1. Choose a clear, uncluttered method.
2. Try to be systematic.
3. Look for patterns. (Are you able to predict the next answer – if so, can you check it by drawing?)
4. Record results in a table.
5. Are you able to make more predictions and extend the table?
6. If you have found a rule can you write it out in words?
7. Are you able to write the rule using algebra?
8. Check the rule.

Example This diagram (Figure 7.5) shows three patterns of white squares surrounding black squares. Draw the fourth pattern.

Complete the table (shown as Figure 7.6).

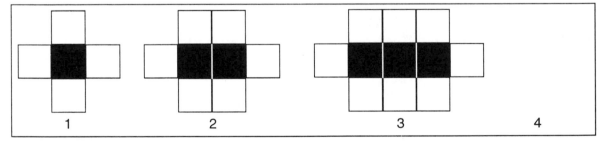

Figure 7.5: Complete the pattern exercise (white and black squares)

Complete the table		The completed table	
black (b)	**white (w)**	**black (b)**	**white (w)**
1	4	1	4
2	6	2	6
3	8	3	8
		Prediction 4	10
		Prediction 5	12
		Prediction 20	Algebra Check 42
		Prediction 100	Algebra Check 202

Figure 7.6: Predicting the patterns

The rule: The white squares are increasing by 2 each time there is another black square, i.e. × 2.

Look at the first case

1 black   4 white
$(1 \times 2) + 2 = 4$

(× by 2 leaves me 2 short so I have to add 2 on)

2 black   6 white
$(2 \times 2) + 2 = 6$ (this seems to be working)
3 black   8 white
$(3 \times 2) + 2 = 8$ (this is correct)

I will try 10 black squares

$(10 \times 2) + 2 = 22$ (I will check this with drawing)

For 100 black squares

$(100 \times 2) + 2 = 202$

To apply an algebraic rule I will substitute b(black) and w(white) into the equation.

$(b \times 2) + 2 = w$
$2b + 2 = w$

When pupils learn how to do simple investigations, their confidence grows and they can apply similar strategies to solve more complex problems.

Expansion of expressions

When faced with two brackets to multiply together students can be helped by using the following procedure and mnemonic.

Example: $(3x - 4)(2x + 2)$

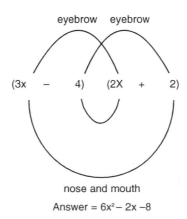

eyebrow   eyebrow

$(3x \quad - \quad 4) \quad (2X \quad + \quad 2)$

nose and mouth

Answer = $6x^2 - 2x - 8$

Straight line graphs

Students need to have each part of the equation explained clearly and then they are usually able to complete this topic with relative ease.

The gradient of a line

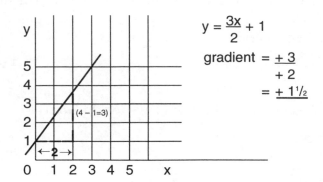

The gradient is the slope of a line in relation to the (positive) direction of the x axis (which tells us how steep the line is). It is easily calculated by finding the change in upward distance and dividing it by the change in horizontal distance. The gradient of a line is shown clearly in an equation because it is the number attached to the x value. If there is just one number there, then the number is divided by 1, if the number is a fraction then that is self-explanatory. If there is no number shown next to the x then it is always +1.

- If the number is positive + then the line will slope upwards towards the right
- If the number is negative – then the line will slope upwards towards the left
  For example,

(a) in the equation $y = x + 3$

     x   means $\dfrac{+1 \text{ up}}{1 \text{ across}}$ positive sloping towards the right

(b) in the equation $y = -3x + 4$

    – 3x   means $\dfrac{-3 \text{ up}}{1 \text{ across}}$ negative sloping towards the left

(c) in the equation $y = \dfrac{-2x}{3} + 2$

   $\dfrac{-2x}{3}$ means $\dfrac{-2 \text{ up}}{3 \text{ across}}$ negative sloping towards the left

Method
Draw the line whose equation is: $y = 2x + 3$

1. Colour the 2x and the +3 in different colours.
2. The gradient +2 tells us that the line will slope towards the right moving upwards 2 units for each unit across.
3. The number +3 tells us where the line crosses the y axes.
4. We can sketch the line now by starting at +3 on the y axis and marking consecutive points in either direction by moving across one unit and either up or down by two units. The coordinates will be (–2, –1) (–1, 1) (0, 3) (+1, 5).

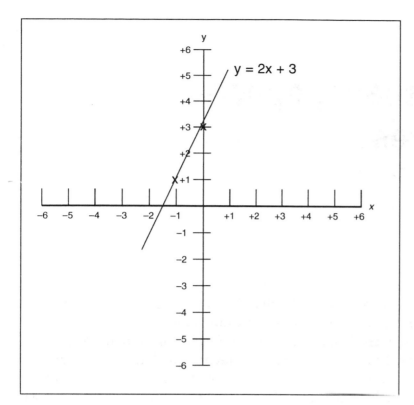

Figure 7.7: Graph of y = 2x + 3

Chapter 8

A guide to shape, space and measures

The topics within this Attainment Target are ones that most dyslexic students enjoy most because, on the whole, they find that they can make sense out of them. Teachers too appear to be happier within this Attainment Target, often using it as a 'soft option' for dyslexic students to allow them to relax. The topics within this category involve shapes which are visual and often concrete which are the necessary ingredients to give success to students with specific learning difficulties. The main difficulty is with the mathematical words used to describe the shapes, their properties and the connections and similarities between them.

Occasionally students struggle with identifying specific lines within other shapes, so may need to use colour filters to cut out the glare in order to isolate the particular figures they need to study.

Other problems that do occur are those connected with:

- Poor organisation
    (a) Blunt pencils causing thick lines to be drawn giving incorrect measurements.
    (b) Untidy pages with no margins, so that numbers of calculations become confused with the main body of the work.
    (c) Badly written '4s' being confused with 'As'.
- Direction
    (a) Measuring the wrong angle, especially with bearings. This is usually when students confuse 'clockwise' and 'anti-clockwise' directions.
    (b) Even when they use the following mnemonics to remind them of North, South, East and West many still confuse left (West) with right (East).

    'Never Eat Shredded Wheat'   or   'Naughty Elephants Squirt Water'

    Often we discuss North and then try to use some method which will enable them to remember that South is exactly opposite. Then we look at and discuss the initials of the two remaining directions, West and East, and realise that they spell 'we'. This can be a better way for many students.
- Language
    (a) Words like horizontal, vertical, vertices, isosceles, etc., are difficult for students to read and also difficult for them to remember exactly what they mean. I introduce the main words which they will come across, encourage them to write them down on index cards with diagrams and, if necessary, put the list on a wall chart. Here

are some words to help (but a fuller list is given in Appendix 1). Teachers may want to use different words with each student.

height	length	width	depth	area
squared	bisect	volume	cubed	parallel
vertical	horizontal	cm²	cm³	units

(b) Symbols used like the arrows indicating parallel lines, and those indicating that lines are of equal length, can cause problems.

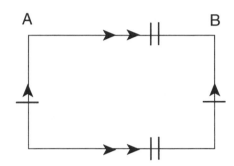

(c) Lines are identified by two letters, one at each end. Angles are identified usually by three letters, the middle one is the angle, the other two are the ends of the lines which make the angle.

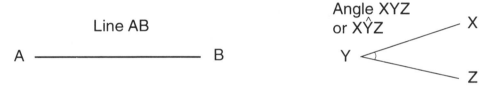

 CAL programs   *Pilot, Snooker, Angles (all Smile Mathematics)* (see list of software)

Shapes

The figures in this chapter are of the different shapes and their properties (Figures 8.1 to 8.6). These visual representations usually help students to remember the shapes, their names and their properties. Students make their own copies of the sheets or have photocopies and should any further notes be required we make them together. These shapes can also be photocopied on to card and mobiles can be made and hung from the ceiling. Using the same idea, three-dimensional shapes can be made showing the properties of each shape and again made into mobiles.

Index cards are made for each shape with the correct words shown clearly. Accompanying notes use key words, if required, and diagrams showing worked examples of area and volume. It is important to remember that each student has varying demands from his notes so their format must be governed by his needs.

Angles

See Figure 8.1.
For the symbol ° read degree or degrees

Acute angles (sharp, pointed): Less than 90°

Right angles: Exactly 90°

Obtuse angles: More than 90° – less than 180°

Straight angles: Exactly 180°

Reflex angles: More than 180° – less than 360°

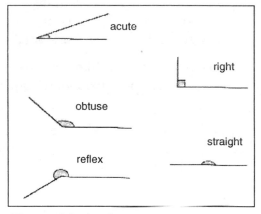

Figure 8.1: Angles

Triangles

See Figure 8.2.
Equilateral triangle

- Three equal sides
- Three equal angles
  (each one 60°)

Isosceles triangle

- Two equal sides
- Two equal angles
  (opposite to the equal sides)

Scalene triangle

- No equal sides or angles

Right angled triangle

- One angle of 90°

Area of a triangle (answer in units²)

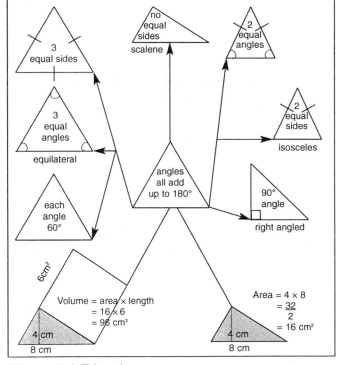

Figure 8.2 Triangles

- *Method 1*
  Multiply the length of the base by the height then divide the answer by 2
- *Method 2*
  Divide the length of the base by 2 then multiply the answer by the height

Volume of a triangular prism (answer in units³)

- Multiply the area of the triangular cross-section by the length

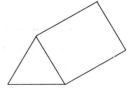

Quadrilaterals

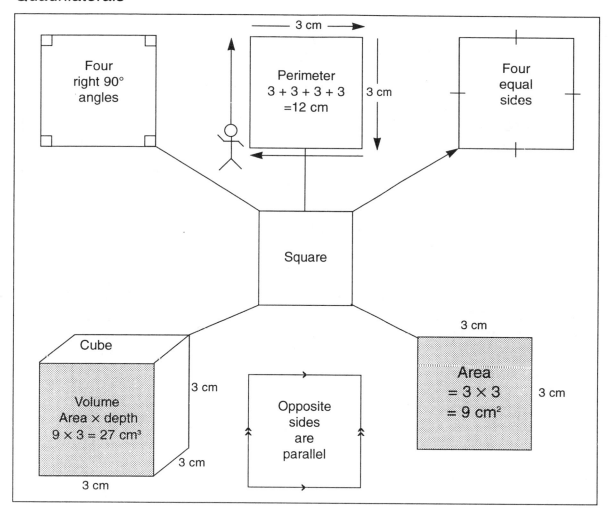

Figure 8.3: Square and cube

Quadrilaterals

Square
See Figure 8.3.

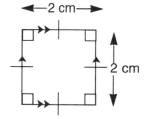

- Four equal sides
- Four equal angles – all 90°
- Opposite sides are parallel

Perimeter of a square (answer in units)
- Add the lengths of the 4 sides
  (Perimeter means the distance around the outside. It can be useful to draw a stick man who is taking a walk around the shape) P = 8 cm
  Area of a square (answer in units²)
  Multiply length by width A = 2 × 2 = 4 cm²
  Volume of a cube (answer in units³)
  Multiply area by depth v = 4 × 2 = 8 cm³

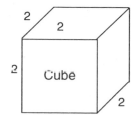

Rectangle
  See Figure 8.4

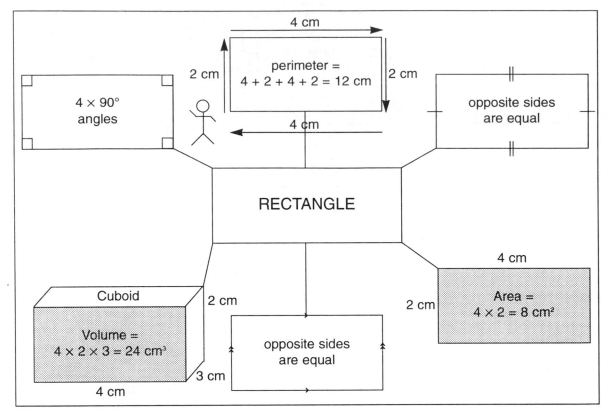

Figure 8.4: Rectangle

- Opposite equal sides
- Four equal angles – all 90°
- Opposite sides are parallel

Perimeter of a rectangle (answer in units)

- Add the lengths of the 4 sides P = 10 cm

Area of a rectangle (answer in units²)

- Multiply length by width A = 3 × 2 = 6 cm²

Volume of a cuboid (answer in units³)

- Multiply area by depth v = 6 × 2 cm³ = 12 cm³

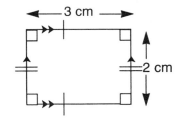

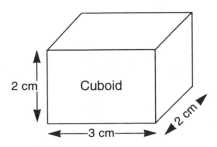

Trapezium
  See Figure 8.4

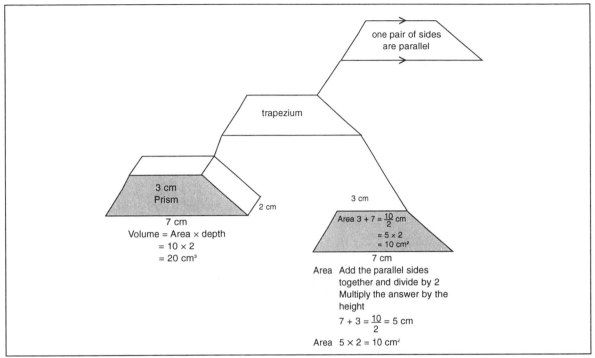

Figure 8.5: Trapezium

- Two opposite sides are parallel

Area of a trapezium (answer in units²)

- Add the lengths of the parallel sides together and divide the answer by 2
- Multiply that answer by the height

$$A = \left(\frac{a+b}{2}\right) h = \left(\frac{3+7}{2}\right) \times 2 = 5 \times 2 = 10 \text{ cm}^2$$

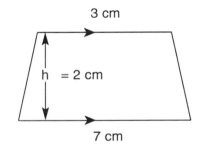

Volume of a prism (answer in units³)

- Multiply area by depth
  $v = A \times d = 10 \times 2 = 20 \text{ cm}^3$

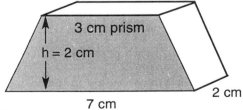

Polygons

Pentagon	5 sides	Octagon	8 sides
Hexagon	6 sides	Nonagon	9 sides
Heptagon	7 sides	Decagon	10 sides

Write the names of the polygon on an index card and encourage students to draw the corresponding shapes. Cut out cardboard shapes and use colour to make the names important. Make big shapes out of vinyl – then students can make floor patterns and in this way begin tessellations.

Finding angles in regular polygons can be difficult. The following method to find the exterior angle of a polygon is one which students seem to understand quickly.

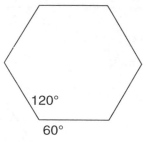

- Draw the polygon and extend a side.
- Divide 360 by the number of sides of the polygon (in this case 6) and the answer is the size of the exterior angle.
- Students can find the size of the interior by subtracting the answer from 180°.

Circles

Words used are:

radius	diameter	circumference (perimeter)	cylinder
curved	height	capacity	mass

Pi π (pronounced pie)

It is important for students to be able to use (*use* because they rarely seem to understand its significance) the Greek symbol π correctly.

- Its value is 3.142 (its approximate fraction value 22/7 just confuses them)
- Press EXP on the calculator to use π

$\pi = \dfrac{c}{d}$ – this is a good exercise to try.

Draw several circles with different diameters
Measure the circumference with string
Divide the length of the circumference by the diameter to find pi.

Draw a circle
Use colour to show the radius, diameter, circumference and the area (see Figure 8.6). Discuss the importance of the diameter being twice the length of the radius and the radius

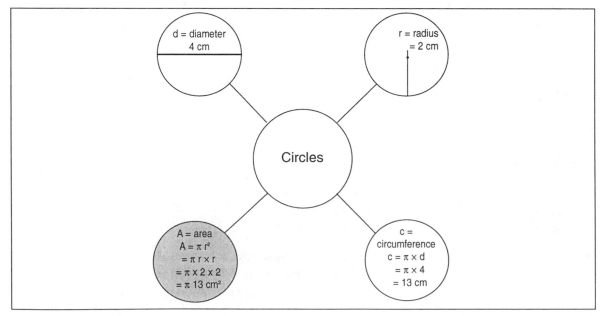

Figure 8.6: Circles

being half (divide by 2) of the diameter. Make an index card stating these facts and put it on the wall as a constant reminder.

Circumference of a circle (answer in units)

- $\pi \times$ diameter (2 $\times$ radius π) $c = \pi \times$ diameter or $c = 2 \times$ radius $\times \pi$

A rhyme to help: Fiddle de-dum
                    Fiddle de-dee
                    The ring round the moon
                    Is π times D

Area of a circle (answer in units^2)

- $\pi \times$ radius $\times$ radius
$A = \pi r^2$

                    The hole in my sock
                    Has just been repaired
                    The area mended
                    Is pi r squared

Volume of a cylinder (answer in units^3)

- Area $\times$ height   Volume $= \pi r^2 h$

Coordinates

Two straight lines at right angles to each other are called the axes. The one which is horizontal is called the x–axis (because x is a cross) and the vertical line is called the y–axis. Coordinates are a pair of numbers, usually in brackets, which describe the precise location of a point on the axes. The first number indicates the x-axis value (across) and the second number indicates the y-axis value (up or down). For example (3,8) means 3 units across to the right and 8 units up. If negative numbers are involved e.g. (–4, –2) this means 4 units to the left and 2 units down.

 CAL programs   *Elephant, Rhino, Ten out of Ten Geometry* (see list of software)

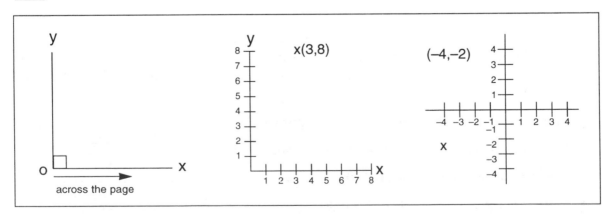

Symmetry

Lines of symmetry

These are lines that when drawn through a diagram divide it exactly into equal pieces (i.e. one half is a true reflection of the other half). If we cut out a shape and fold it in half, the two halves would fit exactly onto each other. Mirrors can be used initially to allow pupils to recognise reflections. Tutors can help by pointing out how specific patterns should look in mirrors. Dyslexic pupils seem to grasp this concept quickly and enjoy it.

Rotational symmetry

This is the description given when a pattern is rotated around a point to identify the number of times the pattern is repeated. The centre is called the point of symmetry and the shape is described as having rotational symmetry.

Order of symmetry

The pattern is given the following descriptions.

If it is repeated 4 times it has rotational symmetry to the order of 4 (i.e. the angle it turns at the centre is 90°)

If it is repeated 3 times it has rotational symmetry to the order of 3 (i.e. the angle it turns at the centre is 120°)

If it is repeated 2 times it has rotational symmetry to the order of 2 (i.e. the angle it turns at the centre is 180°)

If it is not repeated it has rotational symmetry to the order of 1 (i.e. the angle it turns at the centre is 360°)

If tracing paper is used to copy the pattern and turned around a point it allows a pupil to identify the rotational symmetry of the pattern.

 CAL programs   *Alice in Smile Mathematics* (see list of software)

Parallel lines

- Look for the arrows that show that one line is parallel to another.
- Parallel lines are side by side and have the same distance continuously between them.
- A square, rectangle, parallelogram and rhombus all have opposite sides which are parallel.

Angles formed when a third line crosses two parallel lines

- Alternate angles   (Z angles)   are equal
- Corresponding angles   (F angles)   are equal
- Included angles   (C or U angles) add up to 180°

Apart from drawing and colouring in the appropriate angles, students can use cardboard strips to make parallel lines as well as other lines to cross over them to make angles. Angles too can be made from coloured card to make the whole experiment 'real'.

Index cards showing the different angles can be made and filed for future reference.

Direction and bearings

Dyslexics often have difficulty with direction, confusing up with down, right with left, before with after, nearest with furthest, etc. Logo programs on the computer help as they have to give the little creature the 'turtle' specific geometric instructions to make it move in an exact way. They also have to use estimation skills to make correct connections as making the turtle move, e.g. 4 units, needs to be explored to see how far the turtle moves.

If the students have access to a 'Roamer', a friendly programmable floor robot, they can use the same instructions for moving it as they would give to the turtle on the computer. As the floor robot is bigger than the turtle the instructions, i.e. 4 units, mean a completely different length which can also give rise to much discussion. The 'Roamer' also has linking software enabling students to input exact directional instructions which they can monitor to reinforce their understanding. Both the 'Logo turtle' and the 'Roamer' give students multi-sensory practice to help with direction.

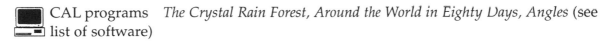 CAL programs *The Crystal Rain Forest, Around the World in Eighty Days, Angles* (see list of software)

Points about bearings

- Draw a North line at the point you are starting *from*. This is most important.
- Measure your angle in a clockwise direction.
- Answer in 3 figures.
- Numbers under   10   begin 00   e.g. 8° is written   008°
  Numbers   10 to 99   begin 0   e.g. 86° is written   086°
  Numbers above   100 are just written   e.g. 267 is written   267°

Scale drawings

Discuss what we mean by the word 'scale', then discuss abbreviations:

represents = rep.   1 rep. 10 cm   or 1 cm : 10 cm

Next use easy numbers to demonstrate:

1. If 1 cm represents 10 cm. Draw a line to rep. 100 cm.
2. If 1 cm rep. 20 km. Draw a line to represent 50 km.
3. If 1 cm : 100 km. Draw a line to rep. 1500 km.

Once this is understood more complicated scale drawings can be used to practise, without pupils having to be constantly reminded of the scale and actual measurements. For example,

Draw your bedroom to scale. (It is a good opportunity to use estimation here.)
1. How long do you think your bed is?
2. How long is the door in metres?

Pythagoras' theorem

Pythagoras, a Greek mathematician, lived in the sixth century and discovered the connection between the hypotenuse length and the lengths of the other two sides of a right angled triangle. The theorem states:

In a right angled triangle the area of the square on the hypotenuse is equal to the sum of the areas of the squares on the other two sides.

The theorem is used to find the length of a side in a right angled triangle when you know the length of the other two sides.

1. Try to find a picture or drawing depicting Pythagoras and talk about the man. Often students cannot remember the word Pythagoras on its own but they remember the picture and with little prompting remember his theorem.
2. The longest side is always opposite to the right angle.

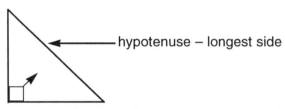

hypotenuse – longest side

3. Present the triangle in different ways.

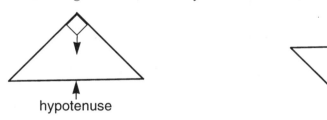

hypotenuse

hypotenuse

4. A good multi-sensory exercise is to draw a triangle with the two smaller sides with lengths of 2 cm and 3 cm so that the hypotenuse will be 5 cm. Then draw the squares on the three sides. Using centicubes make squares of the same size as the ones drawn i.e. 9 cm², 16 cm² and 25 cm² and place them on the drawing. Show that the 9 cm² + 16 cm² = 25 cm² by reshaping the 9 cm² into an L shape to fit around the 16 cm² making a 25 cm² square.

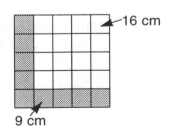

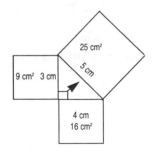

Method
- *Square* the numbers (multiply them by themselves)
- *Add* the numbers to find the length of the hypotenuse
- *Subtract* if you know the length of the hypotenuse
- √⎯⎯ the answer.

Trigonometry

Abbreviations

O = opposite side   **A** = adjacent side   **H** = hypotenuse
S = sine (angle)   **C** = cosine (angle)   **T** = tangent (angle)

Method

1. Identify the sides of the triangle

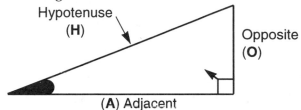

2. Write down   **SOH CAH TOA**   (colour the **H** to emphasise its position underneath the division line)

3.

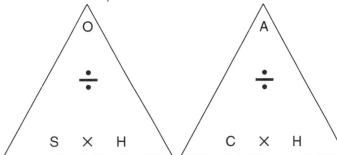

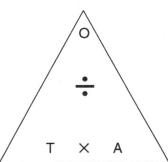

4. Formulae for:

Sin = $\dfrac{O}{H}$ Cos = $\dfrac{A}{H}$ Tan = $\dfrac{O}{A}$

H = $\dfrac{O}{S}$ H = $\dfrac{A}{C}$ A = $\dfrac{O}{T}$

O = S × H   A = C × H   O = T × A

5. Once the formula has been sorted, develop a procedure to use it correctly. Some rhymes to help

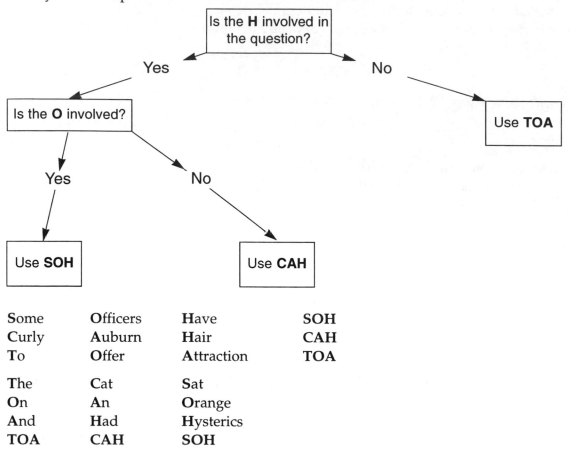

Some	Officers	Have	SOH
Curly	Auburn	Hair	CAH
To	Offer	Attraction	TOA

The	Cat	Sat
On	An	Orange
And	Had	Hysterics
TOA	**CAH**	**SOH**

Chapter 9

A guide to handling data

Graphical representation

Young children using concrete materials are able to understand the principle of block graphs which link up later to bar and column graphs. They need to know that these same graphs can be used horizontally to show the same information. Older students need to discover that some graphs are better than others for representing data, so that in cross-curricular subjects they will be able to select the best graph to illustrate the information they have collected.

Students need more assistance with pie charts. It is important for teachers to consult other teachers working within different faculty areas so that all can agree on methods that are appropriate. In this way students do not feel threatened when asked to draw or read a pie chart in a subject other than mathematics.

 CAL programs *Ten out of Ten Statistics, Excel* (see list of software)

Problems

Dyslexic students do not struggle too much with graphical representation but if they do experience any problems it is usually with the following:

- The words used within topics in this Attainment Target, for example:

  axis   axes   continuous   coordinates   distribution   frequency

  scale   tables   tally   tallying   variable

- The name of a particular graph, e.g. block, tally charts, bar, histogram, column, pie, scatter. (Computer program Excel helps sort out these names.)
- Working out which axis relates to which piece of data (horizontal or vertical).
- The exact values represented on the axes can cause problems.
- Deciding the scale that would not only fit the information but also fit onto the page.

Tally chart
Collecting information is fun and students usually enjoy this activity, but making a tally of the results can cause difficulties. Students forget how to do the five even though the symbols are simple. Checking a list of data means that students are working vertically and

horizontally so the ensuing directional difficulties cause problems for them.

1 = I
2 = I
3 = III
4 = IIII
5 = ЦН1

Different types of graphs

Dyslexic students appear to find working with the same set of numbers and producing different graphs to illustrate the data is beneficial. Initially they draw the different graphs on squared paper, colour them, cut them out and stick them into their books. In this way a good, clear record of the different types of graphs available is made.

Example (see Figure 9.1)

Shoe sizes for 24 members of a class. Draw a tally chart of this.

1	2	3	4	5	2
3	2	4	5	4	4
3	1	4	4	1	2
2	2	3	2	2	4

Size	Tally chart	Frequency
1	III	3
2	ЦН1 III	8
3	III	4
4	ЦН1 II	7
5	II	2

Figure 9.1: Tally chart

Draw a Bar graph, Line graph and Pie chart to show this information and decide which is best.

Probability

Probabilities range from 0 (impossible) to 1 (certain).

Words to know are:

impossible   unlikely   evens (even chance)   very likely   certain

Use the above words to describe some situations.

(a) Tomorrow the sun will rise.
(b) My mother will go shopping on Saturday.
(c) I will be 20 metres tall by tonight.
(d) It will snow next winter.
(e) If I spin a coin it will be a 'head'.

Draw a line to show probabilities.

| impossible | unlikely | evens | likely | certain |

Make up some statements and put them on the correct place on the scale.

Draw a probability scale to be more exact.

0	0.25	0.5	0.75	1

Put the following statements on the scale.
(a) I will win the lottery tomorrow.
(b) Sunday always comes after Saturday.
(c) If I throw a dice I will get a number less than 5.
(d) It will snow next winter.
(e) If I spin a coin it will be a 'head'.

More probability

Probability is written as   P

Students are able to use probability to reinforce their skills in cancelling fractions. The following tips are helpful:

1. If both top and bottom are even they can be divided by two; for example,

$$\frac{12 \div 2}{52 \div 2} \quad \frac{6 \div 2}{26 \div 2} = \frac{3}{13}$$

2. If there are numbers ending in 5 or 0, then they can be divided by 5.

$$\frac{25 \div 5}{40 \div 5} = \frac{5}{8}$$

3. If thereare numbers which the digits add up to 3, 6 or 9, they can be divided by 3.

$$\frac{21}{132} \quad \begin{array}{l}(2 + 1 = 3)\\(1 + 3 + 2 = 6)\end{array} \begin{array}{l}\div 3 =\\\div 3\end{array} \quad \frac{7}{44}$$

I also teach pupils to put the fraction onto the calculator using the fraction button and to press the equals sign which will reduce it to its lowest terms:

$$\frac{13}{52}$$

press 13   fraction button
press 52
press =
the answer is: $\frac{1}{4}$

Note   If the fraction button is pressed again, $1/4$ is given as a decimal fraction   0.25

Spinning a coin

With a coin there are only two outcomes possible: Tails (T) or Heads (H).

Probability of a Tail is 1 out of 2, written as $P(T) = \frac{1}{2}$

Similarly, probability of a Head is 1 out of 2 written as $P(H) = \frac{1}{2}$

Throwing dice

When throwing a die there are six sides so there are six outcomes.

Probability of getting a 2 is 1 out of 6, written as $\quad P(2) = \dfrac{1}{6}$

Other probability exercises

(I have a little bag with elastic around the top which may be used for experiments with probability.)

1. On blank playing cards draw numbers from 1 to 20, colour the even numbers red and odd numbers blue. Put them in the bag, then ask:

   (a) What is the probability I will pull out an even number?
   Students can either work out mentally that there are 10 even numbers or pull out the cards and divide them into two piles noting that there are 10 red cards.
   The probability of pulling out an even number is 10 out of 20

   $$\text{written as } P(\text{even}) = \dfrac{10}{20}$$

   Using the procedures for cancelling down they will divide both top and bottom by 10

   $$P(\text{even}) = \dfrac{1}{2}$$

   (b) What is the probability I will pull out a prime number?
   The prime numbers will be discussed and probably written down

   $$2, 3, 5, 7, 11, 13, 17, 19$$

   Students will see that there are eight prime numbers which are written as
   $$P(\text{prime}) = \dfrac{8}{20}$$

   Using the procedures for cancelling down both top and bottom will be divided by 4 or by 2 twice

   $$P(\text{prime}) = \dfrac{2}{5}$$

   (c) What is the probability I will pull out a multiple?

   - a multiple of 2 $\qquad$ Answer is $\qquad P(2) = \dfrac{10}{20} = \dfrac{1}{2}$

   - a multiple of 5 $\qquad\qquad\qquad\qquad P(5) = \dfrac{4}{20} = \dfrac{1}{5}$

   - a multiple of 6 $\qquad\qquad\qquad\qquad P(6) = \dfrac{3}{20}$

This technique allows me to check whether or not my pupil understands even/prime/multiples, etc. – especially if he is older and I need to be subtle in querying his knowledge of basics.

2. I have some big coloured marbles.
   I put a set into the bag, i.e. 4 green, 3 red and 5 blue.
   We can then do practical experiments.
   (a) What is the probability that I will pull out a green?

$$P(green) = \frac{4}{12} = \frac{1}{3}$$

   What is the probability that I will *not* pull out a green? $\frac{2}{3}$

   (b) What is the probability that I will get a blue?

$$P(blue) = \frac{3}{12} = \frac{1}{4}$$

   What is the probability that I will *not* pull out a blue? $\frac{3}{4}$

The student is also able to test this outcome by experimenting. He puts his hand into the bag four times, recording the colour of the marble he has pulled out. This is done several times and the colour recorded. He then counts up the number of times he has pulled out a blue and divides it by the total number of times he has done the experiment. This should reinforce his first answer.

Many other questions can be done with these marbles. If a student is having difficulties, he is able to take the marbles out of the bag and count them for himself. Later on, more advanced probability is easily shown and the lessons are fun.

Pack of cards
In a pack of 52 cards there are

4 suits	Diamonds	Clubs	Hearts	Spades
	13 cards	13 cards	13 cards	13 cards
	ace	ace	ace	ace
Face or	king	king	king	king
picture	queen	queen	queen	queen
card	jack	jack	jack	jack
Other cards	2 to 10	2 to 10	2 to 10	2 to 10

Questions

(a) What is the probability of getting a 6 of spades?
   $$P \text{ (6 of spades)} = \frac{1}{52}$$

(b) What is the probability of getting an ace?
   $$P \text{ (ace)} = \frac{4}{52}$$

(c) What is the probability of getting a face card?
   $$P \text{ (face card)} = \frac{12}{52}$$

(d) What is the probability of getting a club?

$$P(c) = \frac{13}{52}$$

Sample space

A sample space can show several outcomes.

Two dice thrown and the sum of their numbers is found

+	1	2	3	4	5	6
1	2	3	4	5	6	7
2	3	4	5	6	7	8
3	4	5	6	7	8	9
4	5	6	7	8	9	10
5	6	7	8	9	10	11
6	7	8	9	10	11	12

It is then easy to spot:

(a) What is the probability of getting a 6?

$$P(6) = \frac{5}{36}$$

(b) What is the probability of getting an even number?

$$P(\text{even}) = \frac{18}{36} = \frac{1}{2}$$

(c) What is the probability of getting a number that is a multiple of 3?

$$P(\text{multiple of 3}) = \frac{12}{36} = \frac{1}{3}$$

Many other probabilities can be worked out using the sample space. Students find the visual representation helpful.

Once basic probability has been grasped, pupils appear to progress easily to more complicated problems.

Average

To find the average:

1. Add up all the amounts given.
2. Divide the answer by the number of amounts you have added together; for example:
   Find the average of: 6, 7, 4, 8, 10

   1. 6 + 7 + 4 + 8 + 10 = 35
   2. 35 ÷ 5 = 7   *The average is 7*

Find the averages of the following:

1. 25g, 25g, 30g, 28g, 30g, 24g.
2. Matches in a box: 46, 48, 47, 45, 50, 46.
3. Occupants of cars: 1, 3, 1, 1, 2, 5, 1, 3, 2, 1.
4. Shoe sizes: 4, 5, 4, 7, 5, 2, 9, 5, 6, 3.
5. Hours worked: 10, 12, 8, 12.
6. In a class there are ten boys with an average height of 165 cm, and five girls with an average height of 150 cm. What is the average height of the whole class?

Mode, median, mean and range

Dyslexic students find the first three words confusing because they all begin with the same letter 'm'. Make separate index cards, use colour and word meanings to try to help.

- mode   – most   – most frequent
- median   – medium   – middle size   (large – medium – small)
- 'mean' is difficult because of the 'other' meanings of the word – humble, inferior, shabby, etc. If averages have already been covered then give a clear definition; i.e. finding the mean is exactly the same as finding the average
- 'range' is another difficult word because of multi-meanings. Discuss other meanings and then focus on exactly what is required by the mathematical word and write it down; i.e. the difference between the lowest and the highest value.
- Eventually, when each one has been practised, make an index card to cover all words.

Always arrange numbers in order of size
(a) Mode (most frequent)
(b) Median (middle)
(c) Mean (average)
(d) Range (take the smallest number from the biggest number).

Exercise

Find the mode, median, mean and range of the following numbers. The first one has been completed to show a method of finding answers.

1. 12, 14, 12, 2, 4, 11, 8
    Rearranged in order   2, 4, 8, 11, 12, 12, 14
    Mode   12
    Median   11
    Mean   2 + 4 + 8 + 11 + 12 + 12 + 14   =   63
                           63 divided by 7   =   9
    Range   14 minus 2   =   2

2. 7, 3, 3, 8, 4
3. 16, 14, 19, 21, 19, 20, 17
4. 32, 47, 21, 23, 32, 19, 29
5. 24, 19, 24, 18, 21, 12, 22

Chapter 10

How computers can help

Computers and mathematics

Computers now play a large part in teaching mathematics to dyslexic students. I have often read that computers do not teach, they simply reinforce; but, from my observations, I disagree with the statement. I have seen students learning a great deal from human–computer interaction. In fact, because they often like working with a computer, they do not feel antagonistic towards the machine, which students with specific learning disabilities can often do with a teacher.

These days students often have their own personal computer which they use for hours at a time. They pick up not only keyboard skills but also much information that is now available on CD.

The computer allows a student to demonstrate how good he is working within this medium, often far better than the tutor. If a student is given the opportunity to show his prowess, it gives his teacher a positive start. Then she can build on strengths, not focus on weaknesses (which can happen so easily in mathematics, as students have to complete assessment tests to show just what it is they cannot do well). The fact that a student may have to instruct a teacher on how to access certain information is a boost to his self-esteem. Students often acquire a tremendous eye-to-hand coordination speed, which seems to be a result of practising on either home computers or arcade machines with computer-like controls.

Appropriate software motivates students and shows them another aspect of the topic, often using excellent graphics which today's students tend to expect. I find that patterns are shown well on computers. If a program is good, you are able to stop the program, access, and then input your own information. Also, if the software links up well to the topic being taught, then it is really useful.

What to look for in mathematics software

1. Quick and very easy to access.
2. Has to be user friendly:

    • needs the facility that allows you to go to the exact spot you want, instead of wasting valuable time ploughing through material you do not need;
    • uses language that is not too lengthy or difficult for your student's reading ability;

- uses language which is not too difficult for your student to understand;
- uses instructions which you and your student can remember easily.

3. Should be relevant to the topic currently being taught.
4. Shows clearly the mathematical concept and gives explicit exercises to teach and reinforce it.
5. Uses a variety of ways to explain a topic.
6. Has good clear graphics which are exciting and will hold a pupil's interest.
7. Has a system which allows a pupil to work on his own to practise a concept.
8. Allows a pupil to easily obtain a print-out of his work.
9. Worksheets to accompany the various topics make the programs much more useful.
10. Software should have print-out facilities so that students can continue work after the program has finished.
11. Software which has different levels of achievement, in easy relevant sequential steps, allows students to work at their own pace to enjoy success. Once they know that they can complete a level well, they are keen to reach higher levels which makes programs adaptable for mixed ability students.
12. Programs should be short and sharp, like all mathematical games; reinforcing quickly the particular concept that you are teaching.
13. If the program used games to teach, ask yourself, 'Were they suitable, did they teach the concept and could you exit easily from the program?', i.e. it was not necessary to complete the program to the very end before you could exit (when teaching in one-to-one situations time is limited and having to go to the very end is not always appropriate).

Computers help teachers and students in the following ways.

1. Reinforce principles providing good practice in a novel way.
2. Motivate students because computers are often associated with games and enjoyment (not work). Many students think that they are not working when playing a game and it is often much later when they say, 'Oh yes! That's what we did on the computer. I understand now.'
3. Encourage a student to do better as he is only competing with himself when using software, so the only score he needs to beat is his own.
4. Enable students with sequencing and visual difficulties to produce a piece of well presented work. They do not need to remember symbols or shapes too much as the software will display them on screen, allowing the student to choose. This can lead to meaningful discussion between student and teacher. Where there is difficulty with fine motor control skills simply pressing the right key gives the correct answer.
5. Enable students to develop their own strategies, print them out, review and consider them, and try again in a very short space of time.
6. Encourage groups to share procedures and strategies which in turn can lead to discussion and cooperation.
7. Broaden mathematical concepts with suitable software that introduces different views of a topic that is already under discussion.
8. Enable students who have to produce correct answers in order to move onto the next level to improve both their thought processes and calculator skills.
9. Develop strategies for solving maths word problems.

10. Improve their eye–hand coordination.
11. Give teachers ideas on how to develop number patterns at various levels.
12. Connect cross-curricular themes in mathematics.

Problems with software

Although graphics on computers can link up solid objects and pictures, some of my students cannot see three dimensions when looking at a two-dimensional picture. Objects shown in this way simply become a group of meaningless lines, not the object the picture is meant to represent. Obviously, use of solid, three-dimensional, apparatus in conjunction with the screen picture, allows the software to have the desired effect, i.e. slow, sequential moves through concrete, pictorial to abstract. Once students become used to this they are able to move to a level where they do not need the actual object in three dimensions before they can understand the picture.

Mathematics software for computers can be difficult to choose because of several things.

- Appropriate software for the student might not be appropriate for the computer to which you have access.
- Many schools are still using older machines which will not access the newer programs. Other schools have new machines but find that the software for them is not suitable for their students.
- Sometimes older programs working at a slower speed are more suitable for dyslexic students. However, these good programs for some reason are not updated, so their excellence is lost.

These problems can often create a situation whereby the computer remains in the corner unused. While I have mentioned several of the disadvantages of computer software, I know from contact with the software publishers that work is ongoing to iron out problems.

Different approaches

Mathematics programs for students in school situations appear to fall into approximately three different categories.

Category 1   Programs that deal specifically with certain concepts and topics

These programs are ones that are teacher controlled so that she can choose exactly what she wants her student to practise that day. She can usually select the level she wants, the amount of practice she thinks her student needs and, most often, she knows that there will be a print-out should she need to check on progress.

Teachers like these programs because they feel that they are emphatically reinforcing the concepts they have taught. Sometimes they are afraid that the computer is a little too much 'fun', and deep down they may think that learning should not really be an 'easy' task. I have often heard the 'no pain, no gain' philosophy expressed by teachers, especially in connection with mathematics. If they had more opportunity to stop and study students using mathematics programs, they would see that a great deal of learning is taking place, along with the laughter and friendly competition the programs initiate. If the software that is specifically in this section is well made, then it allows a student to practise, achieve and enjoy success at the same time.

Computer programmers working in this category are now making software that is exciting but still giving students opportunities to do much specific practice. The programs allow easy, direct entry to each part of the software, which is exactly what is required by busy teachers who wish to make the most out of the limited time they may have using the computers.

Category 2 Adventures

Programs which are in this group are exciting adventures that incorporate maths within the story. Often the questions need to be completed accurately or the student cannot move forward to the next part. These can be adventures that are to outer space, around the world, saving the planet or saving a friend in difficulty.

Most students will have had some kind of experience and will be more than happy to show their expertise. In this way a tutor–student interaction begins positively, often enabling a tutor to do some informal assessment of her new tutee. In the program 'Crystal Rain Forest', the student has to give a robot a series of sequential instructions to help the robot to find his way. One of the choices is to estimate how far the robot needs to walk before he needs a new instruction. Students have the choice from one step to thirty. Observing my students I see that the 'inchworms' will usually press one or two, allowing them to keep a tight control over the robot's state and position; while the 'grasshoppers' will automatically select 30 so that the robot will go over the ledge and fall down to the next level! In fact, it could appear possible to detect a learning style from careful observation of a student using certain computer programs!

If a program is selected at an easy level a student will quickly work through it checking that he has completed it correctly. He himself will choose to move onto a higher level to see how well he can complete that one. In this way students are gradually pushing themselves to attain more difficult levels with very little input from a teacher apart from an encouraging, 'Well done' occasionally.

An adventure program, 'Breakaway Maths' by Nelson, incorporates the thrill of going on the rides at the Alton Towers Adventure Park. This CD assesses a student's ability, then, by giving questions at the correct level, gives him the opportunity to answer correctly and move around the park. To go to the very end of each ride, which is shown cleverly so that students really experience the excitement, students have to answer questions on Number, Algebra, Shape and Space and Handling Data. There are textbooks, topic work books and Number work books to accompany the computer software. This package is very useful for teachers working with dyslexic students.

Some programs are able to embrace both of the above categories 1 and 2. One such program is 'Clockwise' by 4Mation. This is quite the best program that I have used because it deals with all levels of telling the time. It is easy to access and easy to leave. The teacher can preset the required level and stipulate exactly how much practice she wants her student to have. Also there is an adventure on a time ship. The time ship has become lost in history and the student has to answer questions to move the time ship through time to bring it back to the present. This allows the presentation of a wonderful time line to be constructed.

Category 3   The National Curriculum in Mathematics

The software in this category is for both classroom and Special Educational Needs teachers but at the moment I am aware of only one program which deals with the GCSE level, i.e. Key Stage 4.

The program first states the Programmes of Study (PoS) with all the appropriate strands. A list of procedures is then shown on screen, followed by the most popular strategies which can be printed out. Should a student wish to add his own strategies, he is able to do this and also have a print-out of his own personal ideas relating to the topic. Worked examples are then shown on the screen but a scratch card can be put on to the screen alongside the worked examples, enabling teachers and students to put in their own numbers and work them out using the computer's in-built calculator. These calculations can also be printed out.

Further examples are given which can also be printed out for the student to work through, with answers being easily available. If a student is struggling with the examples there is a further section showing all the examples being worked through, with appropriate comments to accompany the work shown.

A student can access this program, choose the topic which is giving him trouble, see examples being worked out, practise on his own, check his answer and then receive a print-out of everything he has seen and done. In this way a student can build up a file with all the topics he needs to revise for his GCSE examinations. This fits in very well with the maths dictionary and alphabet box he has been building up over the years, so is one more teaching technique to boost his confidence.

Teachers can pick and choose just what topic they wish to concentrate on and all the examples are there to be printed out and worked through.

Computer Assisted Learning – advantages and disadvantages

As can be seen from the above observations learning as an individual makes students responsible for their own learning, which they can regulate to suit themselves. They see the material, understand the problem and find a solution. If they do this correctly they receive praise from the computer, 'Fantastic!' More importantly they can progress to the next level. This constant feedback allows the student to know just how much progress he is making, he is reassured by his progress and, because he is in control, does not have the anxiety often associated with mathematics.

Although it does not happen frequently students can sometimes continually choose easy material to work with so they are not stretched by the program. If a program is not too well structured students can remain on the same level for too long. Occasionally students find that they are more inspired and motivated from interaction with other students than by working alone.

The advantages of using computers with students with Specific Learning Difficulties far outweigh the disadvantages. Students often come to use mathematics software in their own time as they enjoy the programs. Listening to students talking about a program with enthusiasm makes me realise how far we have progressed in the last few years.

Appendix 1

Word list

	Number	Algebra	Shape	Data	Using number
Aa	about above analogue another arrange average (mean)	across after along always	acute acre adjacent angle anti-clockwise arc area axis/axes	access analyse appropriate assumption average	accurate accuracy add advantage alternate approximate approximately
Bb	belong below	backwards balance before	bearings bisect border broad	bar chart between bottom	back behind bend big bigger biggest
Cc	capacity centimetres (cm) certain correct compass complete compound counter	Cartesian combinations coordinates cube root	calculate centre chord circle circumference clockwise compass compasses concave cone congruent congruence constant converge convex coordinates corner cosine (cos) crescent cross-section cube cuboid curve cylinder	certain certainty chance charts class intervals codes collect column combine conduct consideration continuous correlation count criteria cumulative	calculate calculation cancel centimetre classify classification cold collate collect collection combine combination compare comparison conclude consecutive construct construction convert conversion cost couple
Dd	diagram difference different decimal decrease degree density describe digital direction dotted double	dashed decimetre dimension directed diverging dome dotted down	decagon degree depression depth diagonal diameter dimension divide	data design determine diagram discrete double drawing	define definition difficult difficulties dimension 2D and 3D direct direction disadvantage distance distinguish divide double doubling dozen duplicate
Ee	each edge end equivalent even	equations even expand expansion expression	elevation ellipse enlarge enlargement equidistant equilateral	equal even events evidence exclusive expectancy	early estimate estimation evaluate evaluation even

	Number	Algebra	Shape	Data	Using number
Ee			exact exactly	experiment	expression
				extract	
Ff	face	factor		fair	factor
	figures	forward		frequent	fast
	finish	function		frequency	few fewer
	first				fewest
	flow				flat flatter
	fold				flattest
	formula				foot
	formulae				forward
	fractions				full
					function
Gg	greatest	gradient	geometry	graph	gallon
	group			group	general
					generalisation
Hh	half	halving	height	histogram	half halve
	hour		heptagon		heavy heavier
			hexagon		heaviest
			horizontal		high higher
			hypotenuse		highest
					hot
					hypothesis
Ii	idea	indices	intersect	impossible	identify
	imperial	inequalities	intersection	information	identification
	impossible	inverse	intersecting	independent	inch
	increase		integer	insert	inconsistency
	index		isometric	inter	inconsistencies
	infinity		isosceles	interest	incorporate
	inside			interpret	index notation
	integers			interrogate	individual
	item			issue	inequalities
					inform
					information
					instruct
					instruction
					insurance
					inverse
					investigate
					investigation
Jj	join		join		justify
					justification
Kk	kilogram (kg)		kite		
	kilometre (km)				
Ll	label	linear	left	less	late
	large		length	likelihood	linear
	last		light	likely	long longer
	least		lines	list	longest
	left		locus loci	lower	
	left over		long		
	litre (L)				
	loss				
Mm	magnitude	multiple	map	mean (average)	maximum
	mark		mapping	median	minimum
	metre (m)		mass	middle	measure
	minute		mirror image	modal group	modify
	missing		mirror lines	mode	modification
	most		model	more	
				most frequent	
				multiple	
				mutual mutually	
Nn	negative	notation	net	never	negative
	next		network	next	notation
	number		nonagon	notices	
Oo	odd	operations	obtuse	opinion	observe
			octagon	order	observation
			opposite	organise	organise
			outcome	organisation	

	Number	Algebra	Shape	Data	Using number

Pp	percent
	  percentage
	place value
	position
	positive
	possible
	powers
	previous
	probability
	profit
		pattern
		point
		polynomial
		prime
		proportion
			parallel
			pentagon
			perimeter
			perpendicular
			pivoted
			plane
			pointed
			polygon
			prisms
			protractor
			pyramid
			Pythagoras
				per capita
				pictograms
				pie charts
				possible
				  possibility
				  possibilities
				precise
				price
				probable
				  probability
				proportion
					pair
					pint
					plan
					pound (£)
					pound (weight)
					predict
					  prediction
					prime
					proceed
					  procedure
					profit
					  profitable
					proportion

Qq	quarter	quadrant	quadrilateral	quartile (upper, lower, inter)	quick quickly quotient

Rr	ratio
	reduce
	remainder
	repeat
		reciprocals
		repeat
		right
		rule
			radius radii
			rectangle
			  rectangular
			reflection
			reflex
			rhombus
			right angle
			rotation
			round
				random
				range
				recognise
				relative
				represent
				rounding
					reason
					  reasonable
					record
					regular
					represent
					  representation
					result

Ss	same
	scale
	second
	sequence
	several
	share
	significant
	similar
	small
	some
	sort
	speed
	standard
	start
	stop
		sequence
		spatial
		square
		square root
		symbols
			scale factor
			scalene
			sector
			segment
			semi-circle
			side
			similar
			  similarity
			sine (sin)
			spiral
			spire
			straight
			subtended
			symmetry
				set
				situation
				specify
				spread
				subjective
				survey
				statistics
					score
					select selection
					signs
					slow
					small smaller
					  smallest
					solve solution
					spatial
					substitute
					  substitution
					statement

Tt	temperature
	time
	treble
			tall
			tangent (tan)
			tessellate
			  tessellation
			transform
			translation
			transversal
			trapezium
			triangle
			turn
				tally tallying
				tree diagrams
					timetable
					today
					tomorrow
					tonne
					transform
					  transformation
					triple
					twice

Uu	unitary	units unknown		uncertainty unfair unlucky upper	
Vv		value	vertex vertices vertical volume	valid vector Venn diagram	validate (validation) validity
Ww	weigh whole		wavy weight wide width		weigh weight
Xx					
Yy					yard yesterday
Zz	zero		zigzag		

Answers to exercises in Chapter 6

1. (a) £0.50 (b) £1.01 (c) £0.05 (d) £3.20
2. (a) 476p (b) £4.76
3.

1p	2p	5p	10p	20p	50p	£1	Total Pence	Decimal
3	2	0	1	2	1	1	207	2.07
1	0	1	1	1	0	1	166	1.66
2	1	3	1	2	0	0	69	0.69
2	3	2	1	0	3	2	378	3.78
1	4	1	2	3	2	1	294	2.94
2	0	5	3	4	3	4	687	6.87

4.

£1	50p	20p	10p	5p	2p	1p	Total
1	1	2				1	£1.91
		1		1	1		27p
		1	1		1	1	63p
1		2		1	1		£1.47
3			3	1	2		£3.39
4	1	1		1	1	1	£4.78
3	1	2		1	1	1	£3.98

5.

Item	Cost	Notes				Coins						
		£50	£20	£10	£5	£1	50p	20p	10p	5p	2p	1p
Paper	35p							1	1	1		
Shoes	£24.99		1			4	1	2		1	2	
Tape	£8.27				1	3		1		1	1	
Book	£12.76			1		2	1	1		1		1
TV	£210.00	4		1								
Video	£12.54			1		2	1			2		

6. (a) £1.03 (b) £1.35 (c) £1.70
   (d) £8.12 (e) £25.97 (f) £127.86

7. (a) £85.20 (b) £13.50 (c) £122.42
   (f) £120.96

Answers to multilink exercises in Chapter 7

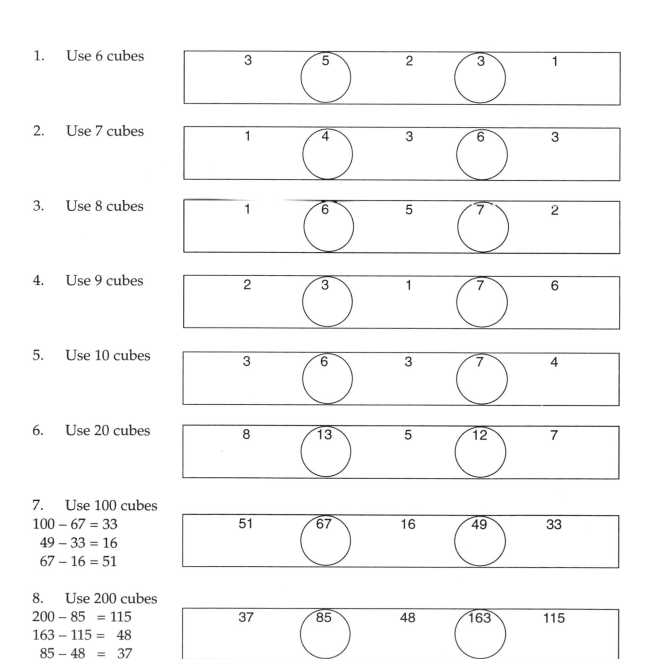

1.   Use 6 cubes

| 3 | 5 | 2 | 3 | 1 |

2.   Use 7 cubes

| 1 | 4 | 3 | 6 | 3 |

3.   Use 8 cubes

| 1 | 6 | 5 | 7 | 2 |

4.   Use 9 cubes

| 2 | 3 | 1 | 7 | 6 |

5.   Use 10 cubes

| 3 | 6 | 3 | 7 | 4 |

6.   Use 20 cubes

| 8 | 13 | 5 | 12 | 7 |

7.   Use 100 cubes
100 − 67 = 33
 49 − 33 = 16
 67 − 16 = 51

| 51 | 67 | 16 | 49 | 33 |

8.   Use 200 cubes
200 − 85 = 115
163 − 115 = 48
 85 − 48 = 37

| 37 | 85 | 48 | 163 | 115 |

Answers to exercises in Chapter 9

Averages (see page 103)
1. 27 g
2. 47 matches
3. 2
4. 5
5. 10.5 hours
6. 160 cm

Mode, median, mean, range (see page 103)
2. re-arranged   3. 3, 4, 7, 8
   mode   3
   median   4
   mean   5
   range   5

3. re-arranged   14, 16, 17, 19, 19, 20, 21
   mode   19
   median   19
   mean   18
   range   7

4. re-arranged   19, 21, 23, 29, 32, 32, 47
   mode   32
   median   29
   mean   29
   range   28

5. re-arranged   12, 18, 19, 21, 22, 24, 24
   mode   24
   median   21
   mean   20
   range   12

Appendix 5

Helpful Addresses

Adult Literacy and Basic Skills Unit (ALBSU), 7th Floor, Commonwealth House, 10–19 New Oxford Street, London WC1A 1NU.   0171 405 4017.

The Association of Teachers of Mathematics, 7 Shaftesbury Street, Derby DE3 8YB.

Better Books and Software, 3 Paganal Drive, Dudley, West Midlands DY1 4AZ.   01384 253276.

British Dyslexia Association, 98 London Road, Reading RG1 5AU.   0118 9668271.

The Dyslexia Institute, 133 Gresham Road, Staines, Middlesex TW18 2AJ.   01784 463851.

Dyslexia Unit, College Road, UWB, Bangor, Gwynedd, North Wales.   01248 351151.

The Helen Arkell Dyslexia Centre, Fensham, Farnham, Surrey GU10 3BW.   01252 792400.

Hornsby International Dyslexia Centre, 261 Trinity Road, London SW18 3SN.   0181 874 1844.

Kumon Educational UK Ltd, 5th Floor, The Grange, 100 High Street, Southgate, London N14 6ES. National Helpline: 0181 447 9010.

The Mathematical Association, 259 London Road, Leicester LE2 3BE.

REM Software Agents, Great Western House, Westover, Langport, Somerset TA10.   01458 253636.

Special Educational Needs (Marketing), 9 The Close, Church Aston, Newport, Salop TF10 9JL. 01952 810922.

Tarquin Publications, Stradbroke, Diss, Norfolk IP21 5JP.

Taskmaster Ltd, Morris Road, Leicester LE2 6BR. Tel. 0116 270 4286
                                                  Fax. 0116 270 6992

Appendix 6

Resources

Beam Mathematical Materials, Barnsbury Complex, Offord Road, London W11 1QH.   0171 457 5535.

Check Cards, P.O. Box 38, Pangbourne, Reading, Berks RG8 7TQ.

Equivalence Playing Cards.   Taskmaster Ltd, Morris Road, Leicester LE2 6BR.

Franklin Spellmasters (Maths Games facility).   Franklin Electronic Publishers (Europe) Ltd, 7 Windmill Business Village, Brooklands Close, Sunbury-on-Thames, Middlesex TW16 7DY.

GCSE Mathematics Coursebook, Levels 5–8.   D. Rayner, Oxford.

The GCSE Revision Guides (Foundation, Intermediate and Higher levels).   The Mathematics Co-ordination Group, Broughton-in-Furness, Cumbria LA20 6HS.

National Curriculum Mathematics, Levels 1–10.   K. M. Vickers.

Read and Write Educational Supplies, Mrs Jean Evans, Mount Pleasant, Mill Road, Aldington, Ashford, Kent TN25 7AJ.   01233 720618.

Roamer.   Valient Technology Ltd, Valient House, 3 Grange Mills, Weir Road, London SW12 0NE.

Sum-Thing, 190 Bag Lane, Atherton, Greater Manchester M46 0JZ.

Sum-Thing Books 1 and 2 (photocopiable worksheets).   Sally Browne, 190 Bag Lane, Atherton, Greater Manchester M46 0JZ.

Time to Time.   Taskmaster, Morris Road, Clarendon Park, Leicester LE2 6BR.

Times Tables (Musical).   CYP Ltd, The Fairway, Bush Fair, Harlow, Essex CM18 6LY.

Times Tables (Rhymes).   Junior Choice Ltd. England.

Times Tables (Video).   Rockhopper Ltd, Freepost CL3713, Dunmow, Essex.

The Maths Pack, R. V. Meer and B. Gardner. London: Jonathan Cape.

Software

Title	Publisher	Telephone	Age
Alge Blaster 3	Ablac Learning Works	01626 332233	10–14
Amazing Maths	The Computer Centre	01487 741223	10–14
		(Fax) 01487 741213	
Angles	Smile	0171 221 8966	
Animated Numbers	Sherston Software	01666 840430	5–8
Around the World in Eighty Days	Sherston Software	01666 840430	8–14
Best Four Maths	ESM Educational Software	0800 378434	8–12
Breakaway Maths	Thomas Nelson & Sons Ltd	01264 342992	10–14
Circus	4Mation	01271 325353	
Clockwise	4Mation	01271 325353	10–16
Connections	Sherston Software	01666 840430	8–12
The Crystal Rain Forest (1 and 2)	Sherston Software	01666 840430	8–14
Don the Professor			10–14
Elephant	Smile	0171 221 8966	
GCSE Maths	Europress	01625 855000	
GCSE Maths	Mathsoft Europe	0131 451 6719	
GCSE Maths	Xavier Software	01248 382616	14–18
Gestalt Time			
Hooray for Henrietta	Lander	01458 253 636	8–12
Math Blaster (In Search of Spot)	Ablac Learning Works	01626 332233	8–12
Math Blaster Mystery	Ablac Learning Works	01626 332233	8–12
Maths Circus (1 and 2)	4Mation	01271 325353	12–16
Money and Shopping	Xavier	01248 382616	8–12
Nature Maths	Sherston Software	01666 840430	7–10
Number Cruncher	Ablac Learning Works	01626 332233	8–14
Rhino	Smile	0171 221 8966	
Sea Rescue	Sherston Software	01666 840430	8–14
Smile Mathematics (1–6)	Smile Mathematics	0171 221 8966	8–16
Space City	Sherston Software	01666 840430	8–14
Space Mission Mada	Sherston Software	01666 840430	8–14
Sum-Thing	The Resource Centre	01509 672222	7–10
Table Aliens	Sherston Software	01666 840430	8–14
Ten out of Ten Algebra Number Essential Maths Geometry Statistics	Ten out of Ten Educational Systems	0113 239 4627	10–16
Time and Fractions	Xavier	01248 382616	8–12
Wizards Return	Sherston Software	01666 840430	8–12
Wizards Revenge	Sherston Software	01666 840430	8–14

References and suggested reading

References

Agnew, M. *et al.* (1996) *Get Better Grades Maths.* London: Piccadilly Press.

Augur, J. (1993) *Early Help: Better Future.* Reading: British Dyslexia Association.

Bath, J. B., Chinn, S. J., Knox, D. E. (1984) *Dyslexia: Research and its Application to the Adolescent.* Bath: Better Books.

Battista, M. T. (1986) 'The relationship of mathematics anxiety and mathematical knowledge to the learning of mathematical pedagogy by pre-service elementary teachers', *School Science and Mathematics* **86**, 10–19.

Chinn, S. (1996) *What To Do When You Can't Learn The Times Tables.* Highbridge: Marko Publishing.

Cockcroft, W. H. (1982) *Mathematics Counts.* London: HMSO.

Crombie, M. (1992) *Specific Learning Difficulties (Dyslexia) – A Teachers' Guide.* Glasgow: Jordanhill College of Education.

Department for Education (1994) *Code of Practice on the Identification and Assessment of Special Educational Needs.* London: HMSO.

Department of Education and Science (DES) (1982) *Mathematics Counts (The Cockrcoft Report).* London: HMSO.

Dunn, R. and Dunn, K. (1987) 'Dispelling outmoded beliefs about student learning', *Educational Leadership* **46**, 55–62.

Godfrey, M. (1997) Personal communication.

Gordon, N. (1992) 'Children with developmental dyscalculia', *Developmental Medicine and Child Neurology* **34**(5), 459–63.

Gulliford, R. (1987) *Teaching Children with Learning Difficulties.* Windsor: NFER–Nelson.

Hart, K. M. (1981) *Children's Understanding of Mathematics: 11–16.* London: John Murray.

Henderson, A. (1989) *Maths and Dyslexics.* Llandudno: St David's College.

Holmes, P. (1996) 'Specific Learning Difficulties and Mathematics: Supporting Teachers, Parents and Children in the Primary Years'. M.Ed. thesis. University of Wales, Bangor.

Hughes, S., Kolstad, R. K., Briggs, L. D. (1994) 'Dyscalculia and mathematics achievement', *Journal of Instructional Psychology* **21**(1), 64–7.

Joffe, L. (1990) 'The mathematical aspects of dyslexia: a recap of general issues and some implications for teaching', *Links* **15**(2), 7–10.

Judah, B. A. (1997) *The Many Facets of Dyslexia.* Santa Rosa, Calif.: Dyslexia Center.

Larson, C. N. (1983) 'Techniques for developing positive attitudes in pre-service teachers', *Arithmetic Teacher* **31**(2), 8–9.

Levine, M. (1993) *Keeping Ahead in School.* Cambridge, Mass.: Educators Publishing Service.

McCoy, L. P. (1992) 'Correlates of mathematics anxiety', *Focus on Learning Problems in Mathematics* **14**(2), 51–6.

Miles, T. R. (1982) *The Bangor Dyslexia Test..* Cambridge: LDA.

Miles, T. R. and Miles, E. (1992) *Dyslexia and Mathematics.* London: Routledge.

Mitchell, J. E. (1996) *Mastering Memory.* Surrey: Communication and Learning Skills Centre.

Newton, M. and Thompson, M. (1976) *The Aston Index: A Screening Procedure for Written Language Difficulties.* Wisbech: LDA.

Newton, M. and Thompson, M. (1983) *Aston Index Revised.* Cambridge: Learning Development Aids.

Orton, A. (1992) *Learning Mathematics.* London: Cassell.

Ostler, C. (1991), *Dyslexia, A Parents' Survival Guide*. Godalming: Ammonite Books.

Pumphrey, P. D. and Reason, R. (1991) *Specific Learning Difficulties (Dyslexia): Challenges and Responses*. Windsor: NFER–Nelson.

Reid, G. (1996) *Dimensions of Dyslexia (Volume 2) Literacy, Language and Learning*. Edinburgh: Moray House Institute of Education.

Sharron, H. (1987) *Changing Children's Minds*. London: Souvenir Press.

Steeves, K. J. (1983) 'Memory as a factor in the computational efficiency of dyslexic children with high abstract reasoning ability', *Annals of Dyslexia* **33**, 141–52.

Vail, P. L. (1993) *Learning Styles*. Rosemont, NJ: Modern Learning Press.

West, T. G. (1991) *In the Mind's Eye*. New York: Prometheus Books.

Suggested reading

Bridge, M. and Hutchins, J. (1997) *Maths Support with IT*. Reading: British Dyslexia Association.

British Dyslexia Association (1981) *Dyslexia, Your Questions Answered*. Reading: British Dyslexia Association.

Burge, V. (1986) *Dyslexia Basic Numeracy*. Surrey: The Helen Arkell Centre.

Chasty, H. and Friel, J. (1991) *Children with Special Needs*. London: Jessica Kingsley.

Chinn, S. J. and Ashcroft, R. A. (1993) *Mathematics for Dyslexics: A Teaching Handbook*. London: Whurr.

Clayton, P. and Lillywhite, C. (1993) *Maths Programs: Using Computers with Dyslexics*. Hull: Dyslexia Computer Resource Centre.

Coleg Normal (1994) *Teachers, Parents and Mathematics*. Bangor: Coleg Normal.

Deboys, M. and Pitt, E. (1979) *Lines of Development in Primary Mathematics*. Belfast: The Blackstaff Press.

El-Naggar, O. (1996) *Specific Learning Difficulties in Mathematics – A Classroom Approach*. England: Nasen Enterprises.

Geere, B. *Seven Ways to Help Your Child with Maths*. Seven Ways Series.

Gilroy, D. (1994) *Dyslexia and Higher Education*. Bangor: Dyslexia Unit, University of Wales, Bangor.

Greer, B. and Mulhern, G. (ed) (1989) *New Directions in Mathematics Education*. London: Routledge.

Hornsby, B. (1984) *Overcoming Dyslexia*. London: Martin Dunitz.

Howson, G. and Wilson, B. (eds) (1986) *School Mathematics in the 1990s*. Cambridge: Press Syndicate of the University of Cambridge.

Ingersoll, B. D. and Goldstein, S. (1993) *Attention Deficit Disorder and Learning Disabilities*. New York: Doubleday.

Matty, J. (1995) *Dyslexia: Signposts to Success*. Reading: British Dyslexia Association.

Miles, T. R. and Miles, E. (1998) *Dyslexia: A Hundred Years On*. Milton Keynes: Open University Press.

Miles, T. R. and Gilroy, D. E. (1986) *Dyslexia at College*. London: Methuen.

Ott, P. (1997) *How to Detect and Manage Dyslexia*. Oxford: Heinemann Educational Publishers.

Pimm, D. (ed.) (1988) *Mathematics, Teachers and Children*. Milton Keynes: The Open University.

Pollock, J. and Waller, E. (1994) *Day-to-day Dyslexia in the Classroom*. London: Routledge.

Reid, G. (1994) *Specific Learning Difficulties (Dyslexia)*. Edinburgh: Moray House Institute of Education.

Reid, G. (1996) *Dimensions of Dyslexia (Volume 1) Assessment, Teaching and the Curriculum*. Edinburgh: Moray House Institute of Education.

Sharma, M. C. (1996) *Math Notebooks*. Framingham Mass.: The Center for Teaching/Learning of Mathematics.

Skemp, R. R. (1987) *The Psychology of Learning Mathematics*. Middlesex: Penguin.

Snowling, M. and Thomson, M. (1991) *Dyslexia: Integrating Theory and Practice*. London: Whurr.

Vitale, B. M. (1982) *Unicorns are Real: A Right-Brained Approach to Learning*. Rolling Hills, Calif.: Jalmar Press.

Walsh, A. (ed.) (1998) *Help Your Child with Maths*. London: BBC Books.

Index